THE ULTIMATE CONSPECTUS

Matn al-Ghāyat wa al-Taqrīb

THE ULTIMATE CONSPECTUS

Matn al-Ghāyat wa al-Taqrīb

ABŪ SHUJĀʿ AL-AṢFAHĀNĪ

Translation & Notes by

MUSA FURBER

ISBN 978-0-9858840-2-4 (paper)
ISBN 978-0-985-88400-0 (epub)

Published by:
Islamosaic
islamosaic.com
publications@islamosaic.com

بسم الله الرحمن الرحيم

All praise is to Allah alone, the Lord of the Worlds
And may He send His benedictions upon
our master Muhammad, his Kin
and his Companions
and grant them
peace

TRANSLITERATION KEY

ء	’[1]	ر	r[6]	ف	f
ا	ā, a	ز	z	ق	q[13]
ب	b	س	s	ك	k
ت	t	ش	sh	ل	l
ث	th[2]	ص	ṣ[7]	م	m
ج	j	ض	ḍ[8]	ن	n
ح	ḥ[3]	ط	ṭ[9]	ه	h[14]
خ	kh[4]	ظ	ẓ[10]	و	ū, u, w
د	d	ع	‘[11]	ي	ī, i, y
ذ	dh[5]	غ	gh[12]		

1. A distinctive glottal stop made at the bottom of the throat. It is also used to indicate the running of two words into one, e.g., bismi’Llāh.
2. Pronounced like the *th* in *think*.
3. Hard *h* sound made at the Adam’s apple in the middle of the throat.
4. Pronounced like *ch* in Scottish *loch*.
5. Pronounced like *th* in *this*.
6. A slightly trilled *r* made behind the upper front teeth.
7. An emphatic *s* pronounced behind the upper front teeth.
8. An emphatic *d*-like sound made by pressing the entire tongue against the upper palate.
9. An emphatic *t* sound produced behind the front teeth.
10. An emphatic *th* sound, like the *th* in *this*, make behind the front teeth.
11. A distinctive Semitic sound made in the middle throat and sounding to a Western ear more like a vowel than a consonant.
12. A guttural sound made at the tope of the throat resembling the untrilled German and French *r*.
13. A hard *k* sound produced at the back of the palate.
14. This sound is like the English *h* but has more body. It is made at the very bottom of the troat and pronounced at the begining, middle, and ends of words.

CONTENTS

المُحْتَوَيَاتُ

CONVENTIONS

المُصْطَلَحَاتُ

Throughout this book, lettered lists are used to indicate things that are required, while numbered lists are used to indicate things that are recommended.

Readers should be familiar with the following terms:

- *wājib* – something which one is rewarded for performing and punished for omitting. It is synonymous with *farḍ* except in a *very* few issues. Throughout this translation, it is usually rendered as "obligatory".
- *sunnah* – something which one is rewarded for performing but *not* punished for omitting. It is synonymous with *mustaḥabb* and *mandūb*. It has been rendered as "recommended".
- *mubāḥ* – something which one is neither rewarded nor chastised for performing or omitting. It has been rendered as "merely permissible".
- *makrūh* – something which one is not punished for performing yet rewarded for omitting. It has been rendered as "offensive".
- *ḥarām* – something which one is punished for performing and rewarded for omitting. It has been rendered as "unlawful".

TRANSLATOR'S PREFACE

مُقَدِّمَةُ الْمُتَرْجِم

SINCE THE EARLIEST DAYS OF ISLAM, the preservation, explanation and dissemination of religious knowledge has been the task of living human beings. Though the Qur'ān, ḥadīth and other bodies of knowledge were recorded soon after the passing of the Prophet ﷺ, reliance has always been upon *living humans* who know and practice, not *inanimate pages* that statically record. When 'Uthmān (may Allah be pleased with him) sent an official *muṣḥaf* [compiled book of the Qur'ān] to the various regions of Islam, each *muṣḥaf* was accompanied by someone who had been assigned the responsibility to teach the masses its proper recitation and meanings. While pages can record meanings, pages cannot recite or explain what they record; pages cannot teach others to recite or explain properly, nor test and—when needed—correct those who err or are mistaken.

Taking knowledge from living masters is nothing new. Before writing, it was impossible to learn from the distant or the dead. Nor is it outdated, as anyone who has qualified for a license or been awarded an educational degree or certificate can confirm. What may be unique to Islam, however, is the command that those who do not know ask those who do (Q16:43), along with keeping an explicit record of the people through which knowledge is transmitted [*isnād*].

Individual Muslims are required to learn the rulings for anything they do in their daily lives. For example, children must learn ablution and how to pray. When they mature, they must learn about the purificatory bath and what necessitates it, and about fasting. If they have money, they need to learn about zakāh and basic matters of commercial trade. When they decide to make Ḥajj or 'Umrah, or marry, they will need to learn the associated rulings. Matters beyond one's individual needs are considered community obligations; enough people must know them to meet the community's needs.

Most Muslims today trace their understanding of law back to schools founded by well-known Imāms, who themselves trace their understanding back to the Prophet ﷺ. This body of Islamic law is known as 'fiqh', which is defined as *knowledge of the legal status of individual actions, derived from their particular evidence*. Its subject matter includes the actions of individuals who are legally responsible: whether an action is unlawful, obligatory, offensive, recommended, or completely optional. Knowing this allows one to carry out what one has been ordered to do while avoiding what one has been ordered to avoid, which results in happiness now and in the Afterlife. It is among the most important disciplines of the Islamic Sciences after the study of fundamental beliefs; it is the cream drawn from the Qur'ān and Sunnah of the Prophet ﷺ. Subsequent generations of scholars continually adapted to the world around them by applying the Qur'ān, the Sunnah of the Prophet ﷺ, scholarly consensus, and legal analogies.

Sunni Muslims follow four schools of fiqh still in practice today. Each school is named after its founder. These schools are:

- **Ḥanafī** named after al-Nu'mān ibn Thābit ibn Zūṭā, known as Abū Ḥanifah al-Nu'mān, who died in 150 AH.
- **Mālikī** named after Mālik bin Anas (93–179 AH), the great Madinan Imam. When the Caliph Hārūn al-Rashīd ordered him to come to relate hadith to him, Mālik's reply was, "Knowledge is something that is sought, not brought." He authored *al-Muwaṭṭa* in response to the Caliph Manṣūr's request for a book of Prophetic ḥadīth. Imam al-Shāfi'ī, who studied under him, praised him saying that "Mālik is God's proof over His creation."

- **Shāfiʿī** named after Muḥammad ibn Idrīs ibn al-ʿAbbās, Abū ʿAbdullāh al-Shāfiʿī (150–205 AH). As a youth he was excellent in marksmanship, language, poetry, and the history of the Arabs. He was a direct student of Imam Mālīk, and was a prodigy in fiqh and ḥadīth. He became qualified to give religious verdicts by the time he was fifteen years old. Imam Aḥmad praised him saying, "The likeness of al-Shāfiʿī to other people is as the likeness of the sun to the earth." His works include *al-Umm, al-Risālah, al-Musnad, Faḍā'il Quraysh, Ādāb al-Qāḍī,* and others. He died in Egypt.
- **Ḥanbalī** named after Aḥmad ibn Muḥammad ibn Ḥanbal, Abū ʿAbd Allāh al-Shaybānī (164–241 AH), the epitome of ḥadīth masters, and champion of the Sunnah. He was a companion and student of Imam al-Shāfiʿī, who praised him: "I have left no one in Baghdad with more understanding and knowledge, and more scrupulous and ascetic than Aḥmad ibn Ḥanbal."

May Allah be pleased with them all.

For most people, knowledge of this scholarly lineage is limited to generalities: the name of the Imam whose eponymous school they follow, the name of a contemporary scholar, the names of a few notables within the school. Students, however, learn the details of their scholarly lineage, including the consecutive generations of scholars, and the relationships between scholars and between books.

Students of fiqh read through a series of texts with their instructors. The first text usually reads like a long set of lists of rulings covering the full breadth of the legal spectrum, but with little detail. Each book in the series adds more detail to the rulings; along the way, evidence, variant opinions, and legal principles are included. Books towards the end of the series include detailed arguments for weighing the various opinions—teaching students how the living masters of fiqh thought.

One of the first names students of the Shāfiʿī school learn is Abū Shujāʿ. His conspectus is usually the first book in the Shāfiʿī syllabus that covers the full breadth of legal topics. The book is known by several different titles: *Ghāyat al-Taqrīb, Ghāyat al-Ikhtiṣār,* and *Matn al-Ghāyat wa al-Taqrīb*. It is also dubbed *Matn Abī Shujā'*. Chances are that the student will read the book at several stages in his study.

In his early stages, he is likely to read the conspectus alone or with a brief commentary, such as Ibn Qāsim al-Ghazzī's *Fatḥ al-Qarīb al-Mujīb*, also entitled *al-Qawl al-Mukhtār fī Ghāyat al-Ikhtiṣār*. Students interested in memorizing the text may prefer al-'Amariṭī's versification in 1225 lines, entitled *Naẓm al-Ghāyat wa al-Taqrīb*.

After reading Aḥmad Naqīb al-Miṣrī's *'Umdat al-Sālik*, he might return to reading the conspectus with a full commentary that includes additional issues and evidence, such as al-Khaṭīb al-Sharbīnī's *Iqnā'* or the *Nihāyah* of Walī al-Dīn al-Baṣīr. If he has memorized al-'Amariṭī's versification, he may prefer its commentary *Tuḥfat al-Ḥabīb* by al-Fashanī.

After reading Imam al-Nawawī's *Minhāj al-Ṭālibīn* or when called on to teach the conspectus to newer students, he might read the various meta-commentaries and marginal notes [*hawāshī*]. These books include al-Jāwī's commentary *Qūt al-Ḥabīb al-Gharīb* and al-Bājūrī's notes—both on Ibn Qāsim's commentary; and al-Bijīrmī's notes on al-Sharbīnī's *Iqnā'*.

Students interested in evidence will find al-Bughā's *Tahdhīb Adillat Matn al-Ghāyat wa al-Taqrīb* useful. Advanced students interested in the evidence and rationale of the various opinions within the school tend to read al-Ḥusaynī's *Kifāyat al-Akhyār*.

This translation is an English rendering of Abū Shujā' al-Aṣfahānī's ultimate Shāfi'ī fiqh conspectus.

5.1 Introduction to the Translation

This translation began in the summer of 2002 as notes for teaching one of my first batches of students. The original translation included the basic text of *Matn al-Ghāyat wa al-Taqrīb* as well as hundreds of notes that I added while preparing for classes. Days before moving from Damascus to Cairo in 2003, I printed a limited number of copies with just the essential notes for friends and fellow students. Since then, I recorded a short audio commentary for the text, and added evidence for nearly one third of the rulings; the translation was also used as the primary text for numerous classes. Unfortunately, the translation never passed through the final stages for publication.

The English text of this translation has changed little since its original print in Damascus. The most notable changes are correcting several embarrassingly glaring errors and the inclusion of the full Arabic text. I have also included notes to point out where later Shāfi'ī scholars had differed from Abī Shujā', Imam al-Nawawī's preferences, and minor clarifications and explanations.

I have relied upon 'Alawī Abū Bakr Muḥammad al-Saqqāf's edition of *Matn Ghāyat al-Taqrīb* for the Arabic text and diacritics. I have altered it in a few places for the sake of internal consistency and when required by the English section headings. An early version of the translation placed the rulings on funerals in their own chapter; this decision has been kept as the audio commentary depends upon this arrangement.

It is my hope that this translation serves English-speaking audiences as an introduction to the full range of basic topics within the Shāfi'ī school of law. Students will benefit most from the book if they read it with a qualified instructor, perhaps after first reading Imam al-Nawawī's *Maqāṣid*. Students who have already read *Reliance Of The Traveller* should find it beneficial for review.

The people who helped me with this project are too numerous to mention. I owe a great debt to the Shafī'i sheikhs with whom I had the honor to study: Sheikhs Abdullah al-Kadi, Haytham, Muṣṭafā al-Turkmāni, 'Abd al-'Azīz al-Khaṭīb, 'Abd al-Qādir al-Khaṭīb, Ali Gomaa, 'Imād 'Iffat, and most of all: Sheikhs Ḥusayn Darwīsh and Muḥammad Ṣulṭān Jād. Students further along with their studies reviewed drafts of the translation and offered innumerable corrections, encouragement, and advice. The following merit special mention: Talal al-Azem, Omar Qureshi, Mustafa Ghani, Muhammad Tayseer Safi, Amienoellah Abderoef, and

Edgar Hopida. This project would be markedly different without the students from my 2002–2003 classes, especially Zainab Chaudhry for her generous help in editing the text. Last but not least, I owe much to my wife and children for their constant support and sacrifice throughout the years.

May Allah grant all who have been mentioned in this preface—and us—His mercy, and may He make us among those who benefit from this noble text. Where I have succeeded, it is only through the grace of Allah; where I have faltered it is from my own shortcomings.

MUSA FURBER
ABU DHABI
13 RAMADAN 1433
1 AUGUST 2012

AUTHOR'S INTRODUCTION

الْمُقَدِّمَةُ

الْحَمْدُ لِلّٰهِ رَبِّ الْعَالَمِينَ، وَصَلَّى اللهُ عَلَى سَيِّدِنَا مُحَمَّدٍ النَّبِيِّ وَآلِهِ وَصَحْبِهِ أَجْمَعِينَ.
قال القَاضِي أَبُو شُجَاعٍ أَحْمَدُ بْنُ الْحُسَيْنِ بْنِ أَحْمَدَ الْأَصْفَهَانِيُّ رَحِمَهُ اللهُ تَعَالَى: سَأَلَنِي بَعْضُ الْأَصْدِقَاءِ حَفِظَهُمُ اللهُ تَعَالَى أَنْ أَعْمَلَ مُخْتَصَرًا فِي الْفِقْهِ عَلَى مَذْهَبِ الْإِمَامِ الشَّافِعِيِّ - رَحْمَةُ اللهِ تَعَالَى عَلَيْهِ وَرِضْوَانُهُ - فِي غَايَةِ الْاِخْتِصَارِ وَنِهَايَةِ الْإِيجَازِ لِيَقْرُبَ عَلَى الْمُتَعَلِّمِ دَرْسُهُ وَيَسْهُلَ عَلَى الْمُبْتَدِئِ حِفْظُهُ وَأَنْ أُكْثِرَ فِيهِ مِنَ التَّقْسِيمَاتِ وَحَصْرِ الْخِصَالِ، فَأَجَبْتُهُ إِلَى ذَلِكَ طَالِبًا لِلثَّوَابِ رَاغِبًا إِلَى اللهِ تَعَالَى فِي التَّوْفِيقِ لِلصَّوَابِ، إِنَّهُ عَلَى مَا يَشَاءُ قَدِيرٌ وَبِعِبَادِهِ لَطِيفٌ خَبِيرٌ.

All praise is to Allah, Lord of the Worlds. May the blessings of Allah be upon our liegelord the Prophet Muḥammad, and upon his pure household and his companions, one and all.

The judge Abū Shujāʿ ibn al-Ḥusayn ibn Aḥmad al-Aṣfāhānī (may Allah Most High grant him mercy) said:[1]

---

1 Aḥmad ibn al-Ḥusayn ibn Aḥmad al-Aṣfahānī, Abū Shujāʿ, was born in 433 AH. He taught Shāfiʿī fiqh in Baṣra for forty years. He was appointed judge of Aṣfahān, Persia. During the period of his judgeship, justice and religiosity spread. He died in Medina, though it is not certain in which year. He was buried in a mosque he had built close to the Prophet's Mosque. It is said that he lived 166 years without losing use of any of his faculties. When asked about this, he explained that he preserved his faculties from disobedience, so Allah preserved them. In addition to our book, his works include a commentary on al-Māwardī's *Iqnāʿ*. May Allah grant him His mercy.

One of my friends (may Allah Most High protect him) asked me to make a short treatise in law according to the school of Imam al-Shāfiʿī (may Allah grant him mercy and His good favor) that is of utmost concision and paramount brevity, so that it[s meanings] become closer to the one studying it and easier for novices to memorize. [He asked] that I include numerous categories and encompass all properties. So I responded, seeking reward and desiring that Allah Most High grant me success in [doing] the correct thing. Verily, He is capable of whatever He wishes and kind to and knowledgeable of His servants.

1

PURIFICATION

كِتَابُ الطَّهَارَةِ

1.1 *Water*

الْمِيَاهُ الَّتِي يَجُوزُ بِهَا التَّطْهِيرُ سَبْعُ مِيَاهٍ: مَاءُ السَّمَاءِ، وَمَاءُ الْبَحْرِ، وَمَاءُ الْبِئْرِ، وَمَاءُ الْعَيْنِ، وَمَاءُ الثَّلْجِ، وَمَاءُ الْبَرَدِ.

Purification is possible with seven types of water:

1. rain water;
2. sea water;
3. river water;
4. well water;
5. spring water;
6. snow; and
7. hail.

1.1.1 Categories of Water

ثُمَّ الْمِيَاهُ عَلَى أَرْبَعَةِ أَقْسَامٍ: طَاهِرٌ مُطَهِّرٌ غَيْرُ مَكْرُوهٍ وَهُوَ الْمَاءُ الْمُطْلَقُ، وَطَاهِرٌ مُطَهِّرٌ مَكْرُوهٌ وَهُوَ الْمَاءُ الْمُشَمَّسُ، وَطَاهِرٌ غَيْرُ مُطَهِّرٍ وَهُوَ الْمَاءُ الْمُسْتَعْمَلُ وَالْمُتَغَيِّرُ بِمَا خَالَطَهُ مِنَ الطَّاهِرَاتِ، وَمَاءٌ نَجِسٌ وَهُوَ الَّذِي حَلَّتْ فِيهِ نَجَاسَةٌ وَهُوَ دُونَ الْقُلَّتَيْنِ أَوْ كَانَ الْقُلَّتَيْنِ فَتَغَيَّرَ؛ وَالْقُلَّتَانِ خَمْسُمِائَةِ رِطْلٍ بَغْدَادِيٍّ تَقْرِيبًا فِي الْأَصَحِّ.

There are four categories of water:

1. *Pure and purifying, not offensive to use*: it is plain water.
2. *Pure and purifying, yet offensive to use*: it is water irradiated by the sun [*mushammas*].[1]
3. *Pure, yet non-purifying*: it is water that has been used [to raise ritual impurity or remove filth] or has been changed by pure substances that have admixed with the water.
4. *Impure*: it is water in which filth has been admixed while the water is [either] less than two *qullah* in volume, or at least two *qullah* in volume and has changed.[2]

Two *qullah* equal approximately 500 Bāghdādī *riṭl* [approximately 216 liters or 57.1 gallons], according to the soundest opinion.

1.2 *Tanning Hides and Bones*

(فَصْلٌ) وَجُلُودُ الْمَيْتَةِ تَطْهُرُ بِالدِّبَاغِ إِلَّا جِلْدَ الْكَلْبِ وَالْخِنْزِيرِ وَمَا تَوَلَّدَ مِنْهُمَا أَوْ مِنْ أَحَدِهِمَا، وَعَظْمُ الْمَيْتَةِ وَشَعْرُهَا نَجِسٌ إِلَّا الْآدَمِيَّ.

Hides of unslaughtered animals are purified through tanning, except for the hides of dogs, pigs, and the offspring of both of them or one of them [with a pure animal]. The bones and hair of unslaughtered animals are filth, except from human beings.

1.3 *Using Containers*

(فَصْلٌ) وَلَا يَجُوزُ اسْتِعْمَالُ أَوَانِي الذَّهَبِ وَالْفِضَّةِ، وَيَجُوزُ اسْتِعْمَالُ غَيْرِهِمَا مِنَ الْأَوَانِي.

1 Imam al-Nawawī's preference is that it is never offensive.
2 Water changes when its color, smell, or taste changes.

It is impermissible to use gold or silver containers [*āniyah*].[3] It is permissible to use containers made from other [expensive materials].

1.4 *The Toothstick*

(فَصْلٌ) وَالسِوَاكُ مُسْتَحَبٌّ فِي كُلِّ حَالٍ إِلَّا بَعْدَ الزَّوَالِ لِلصَّائِمِ، وَهُوَ فِي ثَلَاثَةِ مَوَاضِعَ أَشَدُّ اسْتِحْبَابًا: عِنْدَ تَغَيُّرِ الْفَمِ مِنْ أَزْمٍ وَغَيْرِهِ، وَعِنْدَ الْقِيَامِ مِنَ النَّوْمِ، وَعِنْدَ الْقِيَامِ إِلَى الصَّلَاةِ.

Using the toothstick [*miswāk*] is recommended at all times except after the zenith for one who is fasting.[4] Using the toothstick is more strongly recommended in three situations:

1. when the taste of the mouth becomes stale as a result of not eating, or something else;
2. when getting up after sleeping; and
3. right before praying.

1.5 *Ablution*

1.5.1 Obligatory Actions

(فَصْلٌ) وَفُرُوضُ الْوُضُوءِ سِتَّةُ أَشْيَاءَ: النِّيَّةُ عِنْدَ غَسْلِ الْوَجْهِ، وَغَسْلُ الْوَجْهِ، وَغَسْلُ الْيَدَيْنِ إِلَى الْمِرْفَقَيْنِ، وَمَسْحُ بَعْضِ الرَّأْسِ، وَغَسْلُ الرِّجْلَيْنِ إِلَى الْكَعْبَيْنِ، وَالتَّرْتِيبُ عَلَى مَا ذَكَرْنَاهُ.

---

3 Containers here is understood to include dishes, platters and cups, though the general prohibition extends to instruments, implements, utensils, devices, and the like.

4 Imam al-Nawawī's preference is that it is never offensive.

Six actions are obligatory:

a. intention just as one begins to wash the face;
b. washing the face;
c. washing the hands up to [and including] the elbows;
d. wiping a portion of the head;
e. washing the feet up to [and including] the ankles and
f. doing the above in the order they were mentioned.

1.5.2 Recommended Actions

وَسُنَنُهُ عَشَرَةُ أَشْيَاءَ: التَّسْمِيَةُ، وَغَسْلُ الْكَفَّيْنِ قَبْلَ إِدْخَالِهِمَا الْإِنَاءَ، وَالْمَضْمَضَةُ، وَالِاسْتِنْشَاقُ، وَمَسْحُ جَمِيعِ الرَّأْسِ، وَمَسْحُ أُذُنَيْهِ ظَاهِرَهُمَا وَبَاطِنَهُمَا بِمَاءٍ جَدِيدٍ، وَتَخْلِيلُ اللِّحْيَةِ الْكَثَّةِ، وَتَخْلِيلُ أَصَابِعِ الرِّجْلَيْنِ وَالْيَدَيْنِ، وَتَقْدِيمُ الْيُمْنَى عَلَى الْيُسْرَى، وَالطَّهَارَةُ ثَلَاثًا ثَلَاثًا، وَالْمُوَالَاةُ.

Ten actions are recommended:

1. saying *bismi llāhi r-raḥmāni r-raḥīm*;
2. washing the hands before putting them into the vessel [containing the water]
3. rinsing the mouth and nose;
4. wiping the head in its entirety;
5. wiping the outer and inner parts of the ears using new water;
6. combing a thick beard with one's wet fingers;
7. running wet fingers between the fingers and toes;
8. washing the right [limb before the left];
9. performing the actions three times; and
10. performing the actions consecutively.

1.5.3 Cleaning Oneself

(فَصْلٌ) وَالِاسْتِنْجَاءُ وَاجِبٌ من البول والغائط. وَالْأَفْضَلُ أَنْ يَسْتَنْجِيَ بِالْأَحْجَارِ ثُمَّ يُتْبِعُهَا بِالْمَاءِ، وَيَجُوزُ أَنْ يَقْتَصِرَ عَلَى الْمَاءِ أَوْ عَلَى ثَلَاثَةِ أَحْجَارٍ يُنْقِي بِهِنَّ الْمَحَلَّ، فَإِذَا أَرَادَ الِاقْتِصَارَ عَلَى أَحَدِهِمَا فَالْمَاءُ أَفْضَلُ.

Cleaning oneself from urine and feces is obligatory. It is best to do so using stones and then with water. It is permissible to limit oneself to using [either] water or three stones to clean the affected area. If one wishes to limit oneself to using just water or three stones each of which clean the affected area, then water is better.

1.5.4 Relieving Oneself

وَيَجْتَنِبُ اسْتِقْبَالَ الْقِبْلَةِ وَاسْتِدْبَارَهَا فِي الصَّحْرَاءِ، وَيَجْتَنِبُ الْبَوْلَ وَالْغَائِطَ فِي الْمَاءِ الرَّاكِدِ، وَتَحْتَ الشَّجَرَةِ الْمُثْمِرَةِ، وَفِي الطَّرِيقِ، وَالظِّلِّ، وَالثَّقْبِ. وَلَا يَتَكَلَّمُ عَلَى الْبَوْلِ وَالْغَائِطِ. وَلَا يَسْتَقْبِلُ الشَّمْسَ وَالْقَمَرَ وَلَا يَسْتَدْبِرُهُمَا.

[When relieving oneself] one must avoid facing or turning one's back toward the direction of prayer when in vacant areas.

[Out of good manners,] one avoids urinating and defecating in stagnant water, below fruit-bearing trees, on paths, in shade and into holes. One does not speak while urinating or defecating, and one does not face the sun or the moon, nor turn one's back toward them.[5]

5 According to Imam al-Nawawī's various books, neither is offensive.

1.5.5 Ablution Invalidators

(فَصْلٌ) وَالَّذِي يَنْقُضُ الْوُضُوءَ سِتَّةُ أَشْيَاءَ: مَا خَرَجَ مِنْ السَّبِيلَيْنِ، وَالنَّوْمُ عَلَى غَيْرِ هَيْئَةِ الْمُتَمَكِّنِ، وَزَوَالُ الْعَقْلِ بِسُكْرٍ أَوْ مَرَضٍ، وَلَمْسُ الرَّجُلِ الْمَرْأَةَ الْأَجْنَبِيَّةَ مِنْ غَيْرِ حَائِلٍ، وَمَسُّ فَرْجِ الْآدَمِيِّ بِبَاطِنِ الْكَفِّ، وَمَسُّ حَلْقَةِ دُبُرِهِ عَلَى الْجَدِيدِ.

Six things invalidate ablution:

1. anything exiting from the private parts;
2. sleeping while one's buttocks are not firmly seated;
3. losing consciousness due to intoxication or sickness;
4. direct skin contact between a male and an unrelated woman;
5. touching a human's genitals with the palm; and
6. touching one's anus, according to the new school.[6]

1.6 *The Purificatory Bath*

1.6.1 What Necessitates the Purificatory Bath

(فَصْلٌ) وَالَّذِي يُوجِبُ الْغُسْلَ سِتَّةُ أَشْيَاءَ، ثَلَاثَةٌ تَشْتَرِكُ فِيهَا الرِّجَالُ وَالنِّسَاءُ، وَهِيَ: الْتِقَاءُ الْخِتَانَيْنِ وَإِنْزَالُ الْمَنِيِّ وَالْمَوْتُ. وَثَلَاثَةٌ تَخْتَصُّ بِهَا النِّسَاءُ، وَهِيَ: الْحَيْضُ وَالنِّفَاسُ وَالْوِلَادَةُ.

Six occasions necessitate the purificatory bath [*ghusl*]. Three apply to [both] men and women:

1. intercourse;
2. ejaculation of sexual fluid; and
3. death.

6 Imam al-Shāfiʿī's "new school" refers to his opinions after moving to Egypt. His "old school" refers to his opinions prior to this move. The new school is followed on all but approximately seventeen issues.

Three things are specific to women:

4. menstruation;
5. postnatal bleeding; and
6. giving birth.

1.6.2 Obligatory Actions

(فَصْلٌ) وَفَرَائِضُ الْغُسْلِ ثَلَاثَةُ أَشْيَاءَ: النِّيَّةُ، وَإِزَالَةُ النَّجَاسَةِ إِنْ كَانَتْ عَلَى بَدَنِهِ، وَإِيصَالُ الْمَاءِ إِلَى جَمِيعِ الشَّعْرِ وَالْبَشَرَةِ.

It has three obligatory actions:

a. intention;
b. removing filth from one's body, if any;[7] and
c. water reaching every part of the hair and skin.

1.6.3 Recommended Actions

وَسُنَنُهُ خَمْسَةُ أَشْيَاءَ: التَّسْمِيَةُ، وَالْوُضُوءُ قَبْلَهُ، وَإِمْرَارُ الْيَدِ عَلَى الْجَسَدِ، وَالْمُوَالَاةُ، وَتَقْدِيمُ الْيُمْنَى عَلَى الْيُسْرَى.

It has five recommended actions:

1. saying *bismi llāhi r-raḥmāni r-raḥīm*;
2. making ablution beforehand;
3. rubbing the hand over the body;
4. performing the actions consecutively; and
5. washing the right [side] first.

7 This agrees with Imam al-Rāfiʿī. According to Imam al-Nawawī, one washing lifts the state of major ritual impurity and the impurity itself provided that the substance itself has been removed.

1.6.4 Recommended Baths

(فَصْلٌ) وَالاِغْتِسَالَاتُ المَسْنُونَةُ سَبْعَةَ عَشَرَ غُسْلًا: غُسْلُ الجُمُعَةِ، وَغُسْلُ العِيدَيْنِ، وَالاِسْتِسْقَاءِ، وَالخُسُوفِ، وَالكُسُوفِ، وَالغُسْلُ مِنْ غُسْلِ المَيِّتِ، وَغُسْلُ الكَافِرِ إِذَا أَسْلَمَ، وَالمَجْنُونِ وَالمُغْمَى عَلَيْهِ إِذَا أَفَاقَا، وَالغُسْلُ عِنْدَ الإِحْرَامِ، وَلِدُخُولِ مَكَّةَ، وَلِلْوُقُوفِ بِعَرَفَةَ، وَلِلْمَبِيتِ بِمُزْدَلِفَةَ، وَلِرَمْيِ الجِمَارِ الثَّلَاثِ، وَلِلطَّوَافِ، وللسعي[، وَلِدَخُوْلِ مَدِيْنَةِ رَسُوْلِ اللهِ - صَلَّى اللهُ عَلَيْهِ وَسَلَّم].

There are seventeen occasions on which the purificatory bath is recommended. For:

1. Friday Prayer;
2–3. the [day of the] two ‘Eids;
4. the Drought Prayer;
5–6. the solar and lunar Eclipse Prayers;
7. after washing the deceased;
8. entering Islam;[8]
9. insanity;
10. regaining consciousness;
11. entering the state of pilgrim sanctity;
12. entering Mecca;
13. standing on ‘Arafah;
14. staying the night at Muzdalifa;
15. throwing at the three pillars;
16. circumambulating the Ka‘ba;[9] and
17. traversing [between Ṣafā and Marwā].

8 It becomes obligatory when one of the things obligating the purificatory bath has taken place prior to the non-Muslim entering Islam.

9 The preponderant and relied-upon opinion is that the purificatory bath is not recommended for circumambulating the Ka‘ba. Some versions of the text include entering Medina as the seventeenth entry. See Abu Shujā‘ al-Aṣfahānī, Aḥmad ibn al-Ḥusayn, and Muḥammad al-Khaṭīb al-Sharbīnī, *Al-Iqnā‘ fī Ḥall Alfāẓ Abī Shujā‘*, 2 vols. (Damascus: Dār al-Khayr: 1423 AH/2002 CE), 70; and Abu Shujā‘ al-Aṣfahānī, Aḥmad ibn al-Ḥusayn,

1.7 *Wiping Over Khuff*

1.7.1 Conditions

(فَصْلٌ) وَالْمَسْحُ عَلَى الْخُفَّيْنِ جَائِزٌ بِثَلَاثَةِ شَرَائِطَ: أَنْ يَبْتَدِئَ لُبْسَهُمَا بَعْدَ كَمَالِ الطَّهَارَةِ، وَأَنْ يَكُونَا سَاتِرَيْنِ لِمَحَلِّ غَسْلِ الْفَرْضِ مِنَ الْقَدَمَيْنِ، وَأَنْ يَكُونَا مِمَّا يُمْكِنُ تَتَابُعُ الْمَشْيِ عَلَيْهِمَا.

Wiping over *khuff*[10] is permissible provided three conditions are met:

a. one begins wearing them after being in a state of [complete] purification;
b. both *khuff* cover the area of the feet that is obligatory to wash [when making ablution]; and
c. they are constructed such that it is possible to walk around in them.[11]

1.7.2 The Permissible Duration

وَيَمْسَحُ الْمُقِيمُ يَوْمًا وَلَيْلَةً، وَالْمُسَافِرُ ثَلَاثَةَ أَيَّامٍ وَلَيَالِيَهُنَّ. وَابْتِدَاءُ الْمُدَّةِ مِنْ حِينِ يُحْدِثُ بَعْدَ لُبْسِ الْخُفَّيْنِ، فَإِنْ مَسَحَ فِي الْحَضَرِ ثُمَّ سَافَرَ أَوْ مَسَحَ فِي السَّفَرِ ثُمَّ أَقَامَ أَتَمَّ مَسْحَ مُقِيمٍ.

Ibrāhīm ibn Muḥammad al-Bājūrī, and Muḥammad ibn Qāsim al-Ghazzī, *Ḥāshiyat al-Shaykh Ibrāhīm al-Bayjūrī* [sic] *'alā Sharḥ al-'Allāmah Ibn Qāsim al-Ghazzī 'alā Matn al-Shaykh Abī Shujā'*, 2 vols. (Beirut: Dār Iḥyā' al-Turāth al-'Arabī, 2002), 1:90.

10 A *khuff* is a leather sock. Socks made of other material can be used as *khuff* provided they meet the conditions listed in this section.

11 Other conditions for suitable *khuff* include that the material is ritually pure and water repellant to a certain degree.

Someone who is a resident may wipe over *khuff* for [up to] 24 hours; travelers may wipe for [up to] 72 hours. The duration begins from the point one loses ablution after having worn the *khuff*.

One completes the duration of a resident if one:

1. wipes while resident and then travels, or
2. wipes while traveling and then becomes a resident.

1.7.3 Invalidators

وَيَبْطُلُ المَسْحُ بِثَلَاثَةِ أَشْيَاءَ: بِخَلْعِهِمَا، وَانْقِضَاءِ المُدَّةِ، وَمَا يُوجِبُ الْغُسْلَ.

Three things invalidate wiping over *khuff*:

1. their removal;
2. the [permissible] duration expiring; and
3. the occurrence of something that necessitates the purificatory bath.

1.8 Dry Ablution

1.8.1 Conditions

(فَصْلٌ) وَشَرَائِطُ التَّيَمُّمِ خَمْسَةُ أَشْيَاءَ: وُجُودُ الْعُذْرِ بِسَفَرٍ أَوْ مَرَضٍ، وَدُخُولُ وَقْتِ الصَّلَاةِ، وَطَلَبُ المَاءِ، وَتَعَذُّرُ اسْتِعْمَالِهِ وَإِعْوَازُهُ بَعْدَ الطَّلَبِ، التُّرَابُ الطَّاهِرُ لَهُ غُبَارٌ، فَإِنْ خَالَطَهُ جِصٌّ أَوْ رَمْلٌ لَمْ يُجْزِ.

There are five conditions for making dry ablution [*tayammum*]:

a. the existence of an excuse because of traveling or sickness;
b. the time of prayer having entered;
c. seeking water;

d. an excuse or the incapacity to use water after seeking it; and
e. the existence of pure earth containing dirt, and if it is mixed with gypsum or sand it does not suffice.[12]

1.8.2 Obligatory Actions

وفَرَائِضُهُ أَرْبَعَةُ أَشْيَاءَ: النِّيَّةُ، وَمَسْحُ الْوَجْهِ، وَمَسْحُ الْيَدَيْنِ مَعَ الْمِرْفَقَيْنِ، وَالتَّرْتِيبُ.

It has four obligatory actions:

a. intention;
b. wiping the face;
c. wiping the hands [up to and] including the elbows; and
d. its order.[13]

1.8.3 Recommended Actions

وَسُنَنُهُ ثَلَاثَةُ أَشْيَاءَ: التَّسْمِيَةُ، وَتَقْدِيمُ الْيُمْنَى عَلَى الْيُسْرَى، وَالْمُوَالَاةُ.

It has three recommended actions:

1. saying *bismi llāhi r-raḥmāni r-raḥīm*;
2. wiping the right [limb] before the left; and
3. performing the actions consecutively.

---

12 Dust mixed with sand suffices when the sand is coarse enough that it does not prevent the dirt from reaching the skin. See Abu Shujāʿ al-Aṣfahānī, Aḥmad ibn al-Ḥusayn, Muḥammad ibn Qāsim al-Ghazzī, and Muḥammad al-Nawawī al-Jāwī, *Qūt al-Ḥabīb al-Gharīb* (Cairo: Maṭbaʿ Muṣṭafā al-Bābī al-Ḥalabī, 1357 AH/1938 CE), pp 22–23.

13 In addition to these, one must also convey the earth from a place other than one's own person using one's own hands. See al-Jāwī, et al, *Qūt al-Ḥabīb al-Gharīb,* 24.

1.8.4 Invalidators

وَالَّذِي يُبْطِلُ التَّيَمُّمَ ثَلَاثَةُ أَشْيَاءَ: مَا أَبْطَلَ الْوُضُوءَ، وَرُؤْيَةُ الْمَاءِ فِي غَيْرِ وَقْتِ الصَّلَاةِ، وَالرِّدَّةُ.

Three things invalidate dry ablution:

1. anything that invalidates ablution;
2. seeing [or finding] water before praying; and
3. apostasy [May Allah protect us!].

1.8.5 Splints

وَصَاحِبُ الْجَبَائِرِ يَمْسَحُ عَلَيْهَا وَيَتَيَمَّمُ وَيُصَلِّي وَلَا إِعَادَةَ عَلَيْهِ إِنْ كَانَ وَضَعَهَا عَلَى طُهْرٍ.

Someone with a splint wipes over the splint [or cast or bandage], performs dry ablution and then prays. He is not required to repeat [the prayer] if the splint was applied while he was in a state of ritual purity [and is not on the limbs upon which dry ablution is made: the face and arms up to the elbow].

1.8.6 Dry Ablution and Prayers

وَيَتَيَمَّمُ لِكُلِّ فَرِيضَةٍ، وَيُصَلِّي بِتَيَمُّمٍ وَاحِدٍ مَا شَاءَ مِنَ النَّوَافِلِ.

One makes a dry ablution for each obligatory prayer. One may pray as many supererogatory prayers as one wishes with a single dry ablution.

1.9 *Types of Filth*

(فَصْلٌ) وَكُلُّ مَائِعٍ خَرَجَ مِنَ السَّبِيلَيْنِ نَجِسٌ إِلَّا الْمَنِيَّ. وَغَسْلُ جَمِيعِ الْأَبْوَالِ وَالْأَرْوَاثِ وَاجِبٌ، إِلَّا بَوْلَ الصَّبِيِّ الَّذِي لَمْ يَأْكُلِ الطَّعَامَ فَإِنَّهُ يَطْهُرُ بِرَشِّ الْمَاءِ عَلَيْهِ.

Anything wet that exits from the genitals is filth, except for fluid released during orgasm [*manī*]. Washing all urine and feces is obligatory, except for urine from a male infant who has not eaten food,[14] and it may be purified by sprinkling the affected area with water.[15]

1.9.1 Excusable Filth

وَلَا يُعْفَى عَنْ شَيْءٍ مِنَ النَّجَاسَاتِ إِلَّا الْيَسِيرَ مِنَ الدَّمِ وَالْقَيْحِ، وَمَا لَا نَفْسَ لَهُ سَائِلَةٌ إِذَا وَقَعَ فِي الْإِنَاءِ وَمَاتَ فِيهِ فَإِنَّهُ لَا يُنَجِّسُهُ.

Filth is inexcusable except for:

1. small amounts of blood and pus; and
2. living things which do not possess flowing blood: if they fall into a container and die therein, they do not render it filthy.

1.9.2 Animals

وَالْحَيَوَانُ كُلُّهُ طَاهِرٌ إِلَّا الْكَلْبَ وَالْخِنْزِيرَ وَمَا تَوَلَّدَ مِنْهُمَا أَوْ مِنْ أَحَدِهِمَا. وَالْمَيْتَةُ كُلُّهَا نَجِسَةٌ إِلَّا السَّمَكَ وَالْجَرَادَ وَالْآدَمِيَّ.

---

14 What is meant by "not eaten food" is not having ingested anything other than milk and its derivatives. If the child ingests something other than milk for the sake of nourishment, sprinkling water will not suffice. Because medicine is not taken for the sake of nourishment, ingesting it does not void this ruling. Allah knows best.

15 This suffices once the physical substance itself has been removed.

All animals are pure except for dogs, pigs, and offspring of both of them or one of them [with a pure animal].

Dead animals which have not been slaughtered are filth, except for:

1. fish;
2. locusts; and
3. human beings.

1.9.3 Removing Filth

وَيُغْسَلُ الْإِنَاءُ مِنْ وُلُوغِ الْكَلْبِ وَالْخِنْزِيرِ سَبْعَ مَرَّاتٍ إِحْدَاهُنَّ بِتُرَابٍ. وَيُغْسَلُ مِنْ سَائِرِ النَّجَاسَاتِ مَرَّةً تَأْتِي عَلَيْهِ وَالثَّلَاثُ أَفْضَلُ.

Containers in which dogs or pigs have lapped are washed seven times; one of the washings must include dirt. Other [types of] filth are washed once, but [washing] three times is better.

1.9.4 Vinegar

وَإِذَا تَخَلَّلَتِ الْخَمْرَةُ بِنَفْسِهَا طَهُرَتْ، وَإِنْ تَخَلَّلَتْ بِطَرْحِ شَيْءٍ فِيهَا لَمْ تَطْهُرْ.

Wine becomes pure when it turns into vinegar on its own. It does not become pure if it turns into vinegar because a foreign substance has been added to it.

1.10 *Menstruation and Postnatal Bleeding*

(فَصْلٌ) وَيَخْرُجُ مِنْ الْفَرْجِ ثَلَاثَةُ دِمَاءٍ: دَمُ الْحَيْضِ، وَالنِّفَاسِ، وَالِاسْتِحَاضَةِ. فَالْحَيْضُ هُوَ الدَّمُ الْخَارِجُ مِنْ فَرْجِ الْمَرْأَةِ عَلَى سَبِيْلِ الصِّحَةِ مِنْ غَيْرِ سَبَبِ الْوِلَادَةِ، وَلَوْنُهُ أَسْوَدُ مُحْتَدِمٌ لَذَّاعٌ. وَالنِّفَاسُ هُوَ الدَّمُ الْخَارِجُ عَقِبَ الْوِلَادَةِ. وَالِاسْتِحَاضَةُ هُوَ الْخَارِجُ فِي غَيْرِ أَيَّامِ الْحَيْضِ وَالنِّفَاسِ.

وَأَقَلُّ الْحَيْضِ يَوْمٌ وَلَيْلَةٌ، وَأَكْثَرُهُ خَمْسَةَ عَشَرَ يَوْمًا، وَغَالِبُهُ سِتٌّ أَوْ سَبْعٌ. وَأَقَلُّ النِّفَاسِ لَحْظَةٌ، وَأَكْثَرُهُ سِتُّونَ يَوْمًا، وَغَالِبُهُ أَرْبَعُونَ يَوْمًا. وَأَقَلُّ الطُّهْرِ بَيْنَ الْحَيْضَتَيْنِ خَمْسَةَ عَشَرَ يَوْمًا، وَلَا حَدَّ لِأَكْثَرِهِ.

وَأَقَلُّ زَمَنٍ تَحِيضُ فِيهِ الْمَرْأَةُ تِسْعُ سِنِينَ، وَأَقَلُّ الْحَمْلِ سِتَّةُ أَشْهُرٍ، وَأَكْثَرُهُ أَرْبَعُ سِنِينَ، وَغَالِبُهُ تِسْعَةُ أَشْهُرٍ.

Three types of blood exit from the vagina:

1. menstrual;
2. postnatal; and
3. irregular.

Menstrual blood is blood that normally exits from a woman's vagina and without being caused by delivery. It is black in color, hot and pungent.

Postnatal bleeding is the blood that exits after childbirth.

Irregular bleeding [*istiḥāḍa*] is blood that exits outside of the days of menstrual and postnatal bleeding.

The minimum duration for menstruation is 24 hours; the maximum duration is 15 days. The average duration is 6 or 7 days.

The minimum duration for postnatal bleeding is a single instant; its maximum is 60 days. The most average duration is 40 days.

The minimum duration of purity between two menstrual cycles is 15 days; it has no maximum limit.

The minimum age at which a woman menstruates is 9 [lunar] years.

The minimum duration for pregnancy is 6 months; the maximum duration is 4 years. The most common duration is 9 months.

1.10.1 Actions Unlawful Without Ritual Purity

وَيَحْرُمُ بِالْحَيْضِ ثَمَانِيَةُ أَشْيَاءَ: الصَّلَاةُ، وَالصَّوْمُ، وَقِرَاءَةُ الْقُرْآنِ، وَمَسُّ الْمُصْحَفِ وَحَمْلُهُ، وَدُخُولُ الْمَسْجِدِ، وَالطَّوَافُ، وَالْوَطْءُ، وَالِاسْتِمْتَاعُ بِمَا بَيْنَ السُّرَّةِ وَالرُّكْبَةِ.

وَيَحْرُمُ عَلَى الْجُنُبِ خَمْسَةُ أَشْيَاءَ: الصَّلَاةُ، وَالطَّوَافُ، وَقِرَاءَةُ الْقُرْآنِ، وَمَسُّ الْمُصْحَفِ وَحَمْلُهُ، وَاللُّبْثُ فِي الْمَسْجِدِ.

وَيَحْرُمُ عَلَى الْمُحْدِثِ ثَلَاثَةُ أَشْيَاءَ: الصَّلَاةُ، وَالطَّوَافُ، وَمَسُّ الْمُصْحَفِ وَحَمْلُهُ.

Eight things are unlawful because of menstruation [and postnatal bleeding]:

1. prayer;
2. fasting;
3. reciting the Qur'ān;
4. touching and carrying the Qur'ān;
5. entering the mosque;
6. circumambulating the Ka'ba;
7. intercourse; and
8. seeking sexual enjoyment from the area between the [woman's] navel and knees.

Five things are unlawful for someone in the state of major ritual impurity [*janābah*]:

1. prayer;
2. reciting Qur'ān;
3. touching and carrying the Qur'ān;

4. circumambulating the Ka'ba; and
5. remaining within a mosque.

Three things are unlawful for someone in the state of minor ritual impurity [*ḥadath*]:

1. prayer;
2. circumambulating the Ka'ba; and
3. touching and holding the Qur'ān.

2

PRAYER

كِتَابُ الصَّلَاةِ

2.1 *The Times of the Prescribed Prayers*

الصَّلَاةُ الْمَفْرُوضَةُ خَمْسٌ: الظُّهْرُ، وَأَوَّلُ وَقْتِهَا زَوَالُ الشَّمْسِ وَآخِرُهُ إِذَا صَارَ ظِلُّ كُلِّ شَيْءٍ مِثْلَهُ بَعْدَ ظِلِّ الزَّوَالِ. وَالْعَصْرُ، وَأَوَّلُ وَقْتِهَا الزِّيَادَةُ عَلَى ظِلِّ الْمِثْلِ وَآخِرُهُ فِي الِاخْتِيَارِ إِلَى ظِلِّ الْمِثْلَيْنِ، وَفِي الْجَوَازِ إِلَى غُرُوبِ الشَّمْسِ. وَالْمَغْرِبُ، وَوَقْتُهَا وَاحِدٌ وَهُوَ غُرُوبُ الشَّمْسِ وَبِمِقْدَارِ مَا يُؤَذِّنُ وَيَتَوَضَّأُ وَيَسْتُرُ الْعَوْرَةَ وَيُقِيمُ الصَّلَاةَ وَيُصَلِّي خَمْسَ رَكَعَاتٍ، وَالْعِشَاءُ، وَأَوَّلُ وَقْتِهَا إِذَا غَابَ الشَّفَقُ الْأَحْمَرُ وَآخِرُهُ فِي الِاخْتِيَارِ إِلَى ثُلُثِ اللَّيْلِ، وَفِي الْجَوَازِ إِلَى طُلُوعِ الْفَجْرِ الثَّانِي. وَالصُّبْحُ، وَأَوَّلُ وَقْتِهَا طُلُوعُ الْفَجْرِ الثَّانِي وَآخِرُهُ فِي الِاخْتِيَارِ إِلَى الْإِسْفَارِ، وَفِي الْجَوَازِ إِلَى طُلُوعِ الشَّمْسِ.

There are five obligatory [daily] prayers.

The time for the Noon Prayer begins with the sun passing its zenith. It ends when [the length of] an object's shadow, minus its shadow at the zenith, is the same as its height.

The time for the Midafternoon Prayer begins when the length of an object's shadow [minus its shadow at the zenith] is greater than the object's height. Its preferred time ends when an object's shadow is twice its height. [Its] permissible time extends until sunset.

The time for the Sunset Prayer is a single time. It begins when the sun sets completely, and lasts long enough for one to perform the call to prayer [*adhān*], make ablution, cover what must be covered for prayer, perform the call to commence the prayer [*iqāma*] and pray five *rak'āt* [prayer cycles].[1]

The time for the Night Prayer begins when the red in the sky disappears. Its preferred time extends until the end of the first third of the night. Its permissible time extends until [the beginning of] true dawn.

The time for the Dawn Prayer begins at true dawn. Its preferred time extends until a yellow glow [appears on the horizon]. [And its] permissible [time extends to] the rising of the sun.

2.2 *Conditions Obligating Prayer*

(فَصْلٌ) وَشَرَائِطُ وُجُوبِ الصَّلَاةِ ثَلَاثَةُ أَشْيَاءَ: الْإِسْلَامُ، وَالْبُلُوغُ، وَالْعَقْلُ وَهُوَ حَدُّ التَّكْلِيفِ.

Three conditions obligate prayer. [One must pray if one is:]

a. a Muslim;
b. mature; and
c. of sound mind.

The [combination of these three conditions] is the definition of legal responsibility [*taklīf*].

2.2.1 Recommended Prayers

وَالصَّلَوَاتُ الْمَسْنُونَاتُ خَمْسٌ: الْعِيدَانِ، وَالْكُسُوفَانِ، وَالِاسْتِسْقَاءُ.

1 According to Imam al-Shāfi'ī's earlier opinion, the time for the Sunset Prayer extends until the disappearance of red over the horizon. Imam al-Nawawī considered the earlier opinion preponderant.

وَالسُّنَنُ التَّابِعَةُ لِلْفَرَائِضِ سَبْعَ عَشَرَةَ رَكْعَةً: رَكْعَتَا الْفَجْرِ، وَأَرْبَعٌ قَبْلَ الظُّهْرِ وَرَكْعَتَانِ بَعْدَهَا، وَأَرْبَعٌ قَبْلَ الْعَصْرِ، وَرَكْعَتَانِ بَعْدَ الْمَغْرِبِ، وَثَلَاثٌ بَعْدَ الْعِشَاءِ يُوتَرُ بِوَاحِدَةٍ مِنْهُنَّ.

وَثلاثُ نَوَافِلَ مُؤَكَّدَاتٌ: صَلَاةُ اللَّيْلِ، وَصَلَاةُ الضُّحَى، وَصَلَاةُ التَّرَاوِيحِ.

There are five recommended prayers:

1–2. the two ‘Eid Prayers;
3–4. the solar and lunar Eclipse Prayers; and
5. the Drought Prayer.

There are seventeen prayer *rak‘at* [prayer cycles] of recommended [prayers] associated with the obligatory [daily] prayers [*rawātib*]:

1. two before the Dawn Prayer;
2. four before the Noon Prayer and two after its performance;
3. four before the Midafternoon Prayer;
4. two after the Sunset Prayer;
5. three after the Night Prayer, one [single prayer cycle] which is *Witr*.

Three supererogatory [*nāfilah, nawāfil*] prayers are emphasized:

1. the Night Vigil prayer [*qiyām al-layl*];
2. the Midmorning prayer [*ḍuḥā*];[2] and
3. *Tarāwīḥ*.[3]

---

2 Prayed after the sun has risen and before its zenith.

3 The *Tarāwīḥ* prayer is performed each night during Ramadan, subsequent to the Night Prayer. It is prayed 2 *rak‘āt* at a time. There should be a short period of rest every 4 *rak‘at*. The minimum agreed upon amount among the four schools is 20 *rak‘āt*. One should pray in a group unless he has memorized the Qur’ān and is confident that he will complete it if he prays on his own.

2.3 *Performing Prayers*

2.3.1 Prerequisites

(فَصْلٌ) وَشَرَائِطُ الصَّلَاةِ قَبْلَ الدُّخُولِ فِيهَا خَمْسَةُ أَشْيَاءَ: طَهَارَةُ الْأَعْضَاءِ مِنَ الْحَدَثِ وَالنَّجَسِ، وَسَتْرُ الْعَوْرَةِ بِلِبَاسٍ طَاهِرٍ، وَالْوُقُوفُ عَلَى مَكَانٍ طَاهِرٍ، وَالْعِلْمُ بِدُخُولِ الْوَقْتِ، وَاسْتِقْبَالُ الْقِبْلَةِ.

وَيَجُوزُ تَرْكُ الْقِبْلَةِ فِي حَالَتَيْنِ: فِي شِدَّةِ الْخَوْفِ، وَفِي النَّافِلَةِ فِي السَّفَرِ عَلَى الرَّاحِلَةِ.

There are five prerequisites for prayer:

a. the absence of ritual impurity [*hadath*] and [inexcusable] filth;
b. covering one's nakedness with clothes that are pure;
c. praying on something that is pure;
d. knowing that the prayer time has entered; and
e. facing the direction of prayer [the Kaʿba].

In two situations it is permissible to deviate from the direction of prayer:

1. if there is intense fear; and
2. if praying non-obligatory prayers during a journey while riding [a mount].

2.3.2 Integrals

(فَصْلٌ) وَأَرْكَانُ الصَّلَاةِ ثَمَانِيَةَ عَشَرَ رُكْنًا: النِّيَّةُ، وَالْقِيَامُ مَعَ الْقُدْرَةِ، وَتَكْبِيرَةُ الْإِحْرَامِ، وَقِرَاءَةُ الْفَاتِحَةِ و«بِسْمِ ٱللَّهِ ٱلرَّحْمَٰنِ ٱلرَّحِيمِ» آية منها، وَالرُّكُوعُ، وَالطُّمَأْنِينَةُ فِيهِ، والرَّفْعُ، وَالِاعْتِدَالُ، وَالطُّمَأْنِينَةُ فِيهِ، وَالسُّجُودُ، وَالطُّمَأْنِينَةُ فِيهِ، وَالْجُلُوسُ بَيْنَ السَّجْدَتَيْنِ، وَالطُّمَأْنِينَةُ فِيهِ، وَالْجُلُوسُ الْأَخِيرُ، وَالتَّشَهُّدُ فِيهِ،

وَالصَّلَاةُ عَلَى النَّبِيِّ - صَلَّى اللهُ عَلَيْهِ وَسَلَّمَ - فِيهِ، وَالتَّسْلِيمَةُ الْأُولَى، وَنِيَّةُ الْخُرُوجِ مِنْ الصَّلَاةِ، وَتَرْتِيبُ الْأَرْكَانِ عَلَى مَا ذَكَرْنَاهُ.

There are eighteen integrals [*arkān*] for prayer [mentioned in their order of occurance]:[4]

a. intention;[5]
b. standing when one is capable of doing so;
c. saying the opening *Allāhu akbar*;
d. reciting *al-Fātiḥah*—and *bismi llāhi r-raḥmāni r-raḥīm* is one of its verses;
e. bowing;
f. reposing therein;
g. rising and standing straight;
h. reposing therein;
i. prostrating;
j. reposing therein;
k. sitting between the two prostrations;
l. reposing therein;
m. the final sitting;
n. saying the *tashahhud* therein;
o. saying the prayers upon the Prophet ﷺ therein;
p. saying the first *al-salāmu ʿalaykum*;
q. intending to exit from prayer;[6] and
r. performing the integrals in this order.

---

4 These integrals apply whether one is the imam, praying behind an imam or praying alone.

5 It is obligatory that the intention be concurrent with the opening *Allāhu akbar*. However, Imam al-Nawawī's preference is that whatever custom considers to be "presence of intention" suffices here.

6 The preponderant opinion is that intending to exit from the prayer is *not* a requirement. It is recommended to do so between the two sayings of *al-salāmu ʿalaykum*. If one does intend to exit the prayer before the first *al-salāmu ʿalaykum*, it removes the person from prayer immediately, thus necessitating that the prayer be repeated.

2.3.3 Recommended Actions

وَسُنَنُهَا قَبْلَ الدُّخُولِ فِيهَا شَيْئَانِ: الْأَذَانُ والإِقَامَةُ، وَبَعْدَ الدُّخُولِ فِيهَا شَيْئَانِ: التَّشَهُّدُ الْأَوَّلُ، وَالْقُنُوْتُ فِي الصُّبْحِ وَفِي الْوِتْرِ فِي النِّصْفِ الثَّانِي مِنْ شَهْرِ رَمَضَانَ.

There are two actions recommended prior to commencing prayer:

1. the call to prayer [*adhān*]; and
2. the call for its commencement [*iqāmah*].

There are two actions recommended within prayer:

1. the first *tashahhud*; and
2. making the [*qunūt*] supplication after [standing up from the final] bowing in every Dawn Prayer and in *Witr* Prayer during the second half of Ramadan.

2.3.4 Lesser Recommended Actions

وَهَيْئَاتُهَا خَمْسَ عَشْرَةَ خَصْلَةً: رَفْعُ الْيَدَيْنِ عِنْدَ تَكْبِيرَةِ الْإِحْرَامِ وَعِنْدَ الرُّكُوعِ وَالرَّفْعِ مِنْهُ، وَوَضْعُ الْيَمِينِ عَلَى الشِّمَالِ، وَالتَّوَجُّهُ، وَالِاسْتِعَاذَةُ، وَالْجَهْرُ فِي مَوْضِعِهِ وَالْإِسْرَارُ فِي مَوْضِعِهِ، وَالتَّأْمِينُ، وَقِرَاءَةُ السُّورَةِ بَعْدَ الْفَاتِحَةِ، وَالتَّكْبِيرَاتُ عِنْدَ الْخَفْضِ وَالرَّفْعِ، وَقَوْلُ: «سَمِعَ اللهُ لِمَنْ حَمِدَهُ رَبَّنَا لَكَ الْحَمْدُ»، وَالتَّسْبِيحُ فِي الرُّكُوعِ وَالسُّجُودِ، وَوَضْعُ الْيَدَيْنِ عَلَى الْفَخِذَيْنِ فِي الْجُلُوسِ يَبْسُطُ الْيُسْرَى وَيَقْبِضُ الْيُمْنَى إِلَّا الْمُسَبِّحَةَ فَإِنَّهُ يُشِيرُ بِهَا مُتَشَهِّدًا، وَالِافْتِرَاشُ فِي جَمِيعِ الْجَلَسَاتِ، وَالتَّوَرُّكُ فِي الْجَلْسَةِ الْأَخِيرَةِ، وَالتَّسْلِيمَةُ الثَّانِيَةُ.

There are fifteen lesser recommended actions [*hay'at*]:[7]

1. raising the hands concurrently with saying the opening *Allāhu akbar*, bowing and rising [from it];
2. placing the right hand over the left;
3. saying the opening supplication;
4. seeking protection from Satan;
5. audible utterances when appropriate;
6. quiet utterances when appropriate;[8]
7. saying *āmīn*;
8. reciting a chapter [of the Qur'ān] after *al-Fātiḥah*;
9. saying *Allāhu akbar* when rising and descending;
10. saying *sami'a Allāhu li man ḥamidah* [as one begins to rise from bowing], *rabbanā laka al-ḥamd* [after one has straightened up];
11. saying *subḥāna rabbī al-'aẓīm* when bowing and *subḥāna rabbī al-'alā* when prostrating;
12. placing one's hands upon one's thighs while sitting, extending the fingers of the left hand and closing the right except for the index finger, with which one points during the *tashahhud*;
13. sitting in the manner of *iftirāsh* in all places wherein one sits, but
14. sitting in the manner of *tawarruk* in the final sitting;[9] and
15. saying the second *al-salāmu 'alaykum*.

---

7 The lesser recommended actions are actions that do not call for a prostration of forgetfulness if omitted.

8 In order for an utterance to be of consideration, it must be loud enough that one can hear it; a mute is required to move his tongue. During the Dawn, Sunset and Night Prayers, the imam and those praying individually should recite *al-Fātiḥah* and any additional Qur'ān during the first two *rak'āt* aloud.

9 To sit in the manner of *iftirāsh*, one sits with the left foot below one's buttocks while the right foot is raised up with the toes on the ground pointing towards the direction of prayer. For *tawarruk*, one does similar to the above, except that the left foot goes out under the right shin and the bottom of the left thigh and buttocks are in contact with the ground.

2.3.5 Men and Women During Prayer

(فَصْلٌ) وَالْمَرْأَةُ تُخَالِفُ الرَّجُلَ فِي خَمْسَةِ أَشْيَاءَ: فَالرَّجُلُ يُجَافِي مِرْفَقَيْهِ عَنْ جَنْبَيْهِ، وَيُقِلُّ بَطْنَهُ عَنْ فَخِذَيْهِ فِي السُّجُودِ، وَيَجْهَرُ فِي مَوْضِعِ الْجَهْرِ، وَإِذَا نَابَهُ شَيْءٌ فِي الصَّلَاةِ سَبَّحَ، وَعَوْرَةُ الرَّجُلِ مَا بَيْنَ سُرَّتِهِ وَرُكْبَتِهِ.

وَالْمَرْأَةُ تَضُمُّ بَعْضَهَا إِلَى بَعْضٍ، وَتَخْفِضُ صَوْتَهَا بِحَضْرَةِ الرِّجَالِ الْأَجَانِبِ، وَإِذَا نَابَهَا شَيْءٌ فِي الصَّلَاةِ صَفَّقَتْ، وَجَمِيعُ بَدَنِ الْحُرَّةِ عَوْرَةٌ إِلَّا وَجْهَهَا وَكَفَّيْهَا، وَالْأَمَةُ كَالرَّجُلِ.

Women [with respect to prayer] differ from men in five things. A man:

1. spreads his elbows out from his sides;
2. raises his stomach from his thighs during bowing and prostrating;
3. recites audibly when appropriate;
4. says *subḥān Allah* if something occurs during prayer;[10] and
5. his nakedness is the area between his navel and his knees.

[Whereas] a woman:

1. draws herself together [when bowing and prostrating];
3. lowers her voice in the presence of men who are not close relatives;
4. claps if something occurs during prayer; and
5. a free woman must cover her entire body except her face and hands, while a female slave covers the same as a man.

10 Such as alerting the imam to a mistake, giving a visitor permission to enter or warning a blind person from potential danger. See al-Sharbīnī, et al, *Al-Iqnāʿ*, 149.

2.3.6 Invalidators

(فَصْلٌ) وَالَّذِي يُبْطِلُ الصَّلَاةَ أَحَدَ عَشَرَ شَيْئًا: الْكَلَامُ الْعَمْدُ، وَالْعَمَلُ الْكَثِيرُ، وَالْحَدَثُ، وَحُدُوثُ النَّجَاسَةِ، وَانْكِشَافُ الْعَوْرَةِ، وَتَغْيِيرُ النِّيَّةِ، وَاسْتِدْبَارُ الْقِبْلَةِ، وَالْأَكْلُ، وَالشُّرْبُ، وَالْقَهْقَهَةُ، وَالرِّدَّةُ.

Eleven things invalidate prayer:

1. intentional speech;
2. excessive motion;
3. ritual impurity;
4. the occurrence of filth;
5. exposure of one's nakedness;
6. a change of intention;
7. turning away from the direction of prayer;
8. eating;
9. drinking;
10. cackling; and
11. apostasy [May Allah protect us!].

2.3.7 Quantity of Prayer Elements

(فَصْلٌ) وَرَكَعَاتُ الْفَرَائِضِ سَبْعَ عَشْرَةَ رَكْعَةً، فِيهَا أَرْبَعٌ وَثَلَاثُونَ سَجْدَةً، وَأَرْبَعٌ وَتِسْعُونَ تَكْبِيرَةً، وَتِسْعَةُ تَشَهُّدَاتٍ وَعَشْرُ تَسْلِيمَاتٍ، وَمِائَةٌ وَثَلَاثٌ وَخَمْسُونَ تَسْبِيحَةً.

وَجُمْلَةُ الْأَرْكَانِ فِي الصَّلَاةِ مِائَةٌ وَسِتٌّ وَعِشْرُونَ رُكْنًا: فِي الصُّبْحِ ثَلَاثُونَ رُكْنًا، وَفِي الْمَغْرِبِ اثْنَانِ وَأَرْبَعُونَ رُكْنًا، وَفِي الرُّبَاعِيَّةِ أَرْبَعَةٌ وَخَمْسُونَ رُكْنًا.

There are 17 obligatory *rak'āt*, which contain 34 prostrations, 94 occurrences of *Allāhu akbar*, 9 *tashahhuds*, 10 sayings of *al-*

salāmu ʿalaykum, and 153 sayings of *subḥāna rabbī al-ʿaẓīm* or *subḥāna rabbī al-aʿlā*.

There is a total number of 126 integrals during [these] prayers: 30 during the Dawn Prayer, 42 during the Sunset Prayer, and 54 during the four-*rakʿāt* prayers [the Noon, Midafternoon, and Night Prayers].

2.3.8 Inability

وَمَنْ عَجَزَ عَنِ الْقِيَامِ فِي الْفَرِيضَةِ صَلَّى جَالِسًا، وَمَنْ عَجَزَ عَنِ الْجُلُوسِ صَلَّى مُضْطَجِعًا.

Anyone unable to stand during the obligatory prayers may pray seated. If also unable to sit, one may pray lying on one's side.

2.3.9 Forgetfulness During Prayer

(فَصْلٌ) وَالْمَتْرُوكُ مِنَ الصَّلَاةِ ثَلَاثَةُ أَشْيَاءَ: فَرْضٌ، وَسُنَّةٌ، وَهَيْئَةٌ. فَالْفَرْضُ لَا يَنُوبُ عَنْهُ سُجُودُ السَّهْوِ، بَلْ إِنْ ذَكَرَهُ وَالزَّمَانُ قَرِيبٌ أَتَى بِهِ وَبَنَى عَلَيْهِ وَسَجَدَ لِلسَّهْوِ. وَالسُّنَّةُ لَا يَعُودُ إِلَيْهَا بَعْدَ التَّلَبُّسِ بِالفَرْضِ لَكِنَّهُ يَسْجُدُ لِلسَّهْوِ. وَالْهَيْئَةُ لَا يَعُودُ إِلَيْهَا بَعْدَ تَرْكِهَا وَلَا يَسْجُدُ لِلسَّهْوِ عَنْهَا.

وَإِذَا شَكَّ فِي عَدَدِ مَا أَتَى بِهِ مِنْ الرَّكَعَاتِ بَنَى عَلَى الْيَقِينِ وَهُوَ الْأَقَلُّ وَسَجَدَ لِلسَّهْوِ. وَسُجُودُ السَّهْوِ سُنَّةٌ، وَمَحَلُّهُ قَبْلَ السَّلَامِ.

There are three types of actions that might be omitted in prayer:

1. obligatory;
2. recommended; and
3. lesser recommended actions.

Obligatory: The prostration for forgetfulness does not take its place. Instead, if one remembers it soon after its omission, one performs the action, continues the prayer and makes a prostration for forgetfulness.

Recommended: One does not return to a recommended action after engaging in an action that is obligatory. One does, however, make a prostration for forgetfulness for its omission.

Lesser recommended actions: One does not return to a lesser recommended action after its omission nor make a prostration for forgetfulness for its omission.

If one has doubts concerning how many *rak'āt* one has completed, one takes the certain number (the least [of the possibilities]), prays the rest and performs a prostration for forgetfulness.

The prostration for forgetfulness is recommended. The location of the prostration for forgetfulness is before saying [the first closing] *al-salāmu 'alaykum*.

2.4 *Times Wherein Prayer is Unlawful*

(فَصْلٌ) وَخَمْسَةُ أَوْقَاتٍ لَا يُصَلَّى فِيهَا إِلَّا صَلَاةٌ لَهَا سَبَبٌ: بَعْدَ صَلَاةِ الصُّبْحِ حَتَّى تَطْلُعَ الشَّمْسُ، وَعِنْدَ طُلُوعِهَا حَتَّى تَتَكَامَلَ وَتَرْتَفِعَ قَدْرَ رُمْحٍ، وَإِذَا اسْتَوَتْ حَتَّى تَزُولَ، وَبَعْدَ الْعَصْرِ حَتَّى تَغْرُبَ الشَّمْسُ، وَعِنْدَ الْغُرُوبِ حَتَّى يَتَكَامَلَ غُرُوبُهَا.

It is unlawful to perform a prayer that lacks a cause [concurrent with or arising prior to the prayer's performance] during five times:

1. after the Dawn Prayer until [the onset of] sunrise;
2. from [the onset of] sunrise until its completion and the sun has risen one spear-length [above the horizon];

3. when the sun is at its zenith;
4. after the Midafternoon Prayer until [the onset of] sunset; and
5. from [the onset of] sunset until its completion.

2.5 *Congregational Prayer*

(فَصْلٌ) وَصَلَاةُ الْجَمَاعَةِ سُنَّةٌ مُؤَكَّدَةٌ. وَعَلَى الْمَأْمُومِ أَنْ يَنْوِيَ الِائْتِمَامَ دُونَ الْإِمَامِ.

وَيَجُوزُ أَنْ يَأْتَمَّ الْحُرُّ بِالْعَبْدِ، وَالْبَالِغُ بِالْمُرَاهِقِ. وَلَا تَصِحُّ قُدْوَةُ رَجُلٍ بِامْرَأَةٍ، وَلَا قَارِئٌ بِأُمِّيٍّ.

وَأَيُّ مَوْضِعٍ صَلَّى فِي الْمَسْجِدِ بِصَلَاةِ الْإِمَامِ فِيهِ وَهُوَ عَالِمٌ بِصَلَاتِهِ أَجْزَأَهُ مَا لَمْ يَتَقَدَّمْ عَلَيْهِ، وَإِنْ صَلَّى فِي الْمَسْجِدِ وَالْمَأْمُومُ خَارِجَ الْمَسْجِدِ قَرِيبًا مِنْهُ وَهُوَ عَالِمٌ بِصَلَاتِهِ وَلَا حَائِلَ هُنَاكَ جَازَ.

Congregational prayer is an emphasized sunnah [*mu'akkadah*].[11]

Followers must intend to follow, but it is not required that the imam intend to lead.

It is permissible [and valid] for someone who is free to be led by a slave, and for one who is mature to pray behind an adolescent.

It is not valid for a male to be led by a female, nor for one who reads *al-Fātiḥah* correctly to be led by someone who does not.

Wherever one prays in a mosque behind the imam while aware of the imam's prayer, the prayer suffices, provided one does not advance closer to the direction of prayer than his imam.

---

11 The stronger opinion according to Imam al-Nawawī is that it is a community obligation.

If the imam prays inside a mosque and the follower prays [behind and] close[12] outside, it is permissible, provided that the follower is aware of the imam's prayer and there is no barrier between them.

2.6 *Travelers*

2.6.1 Shortening

(فَصْلٌ) وَيَجُوزُ لِلْمُسَافِرِ قَصْرُ الصَّلَاةِ الرُّبَاعِيَّةِ بِخَمْسَةِ شَرَائِطَ: أَنْ يَكُونَ سَفَرُهُ فِي غَيْرِ مَعْصِيَةٍ، وَأَنْ تَكُونَ مَسَافَتُهُ سِتَّةَ عَشَرَ فَرْسَخًا، وَأَنْ يَكُونَ مُؤَدِّيًا لِلصَّلَاةِ الرُّبَاعِيَّةِ، وَأَنْ يَنْوِيَ الْقَصْرَ مَعَ الْإِحْرَامِ، وَأَنْ لَا يَأْتَمَّ بِمُقِيمٍ.

Travelers are entitled to shorten prayers consisting of four *rak'āt*s [to two *rak'āt*s] provided that five conditions are met:

a. the journey itself does not entail disobedience;
b. the distance of the journey be at least 16 *farsakh* [approximately 50 miles, or 81 kilometers];
c. the prayer being performed [normally] consists of four *rak'āt*s;
d. the intention to shorten [the prayer] is concurrent with the opening *Allāhu akbar* and
e. the one shortening prayers does not follow a resident [or a traveler who is not shortening prayer] [in prayer].

2.6.2 Combining

وَيَجُوزُ لِلْمُسَافِرِ أَنْ يَجْمَعَ بَيْنَ الظُّهْرِ وَالْعَصْرِ فِي وَقْتِ أَيِّهِمَا شَاءَ، وَبَيْنَ الْمَغْرِبِ وَالْعِشَاءِ فِي وَقْتِ أَيِّهِمَا شَاءَ. وَيَجُوزُ لِلْحَاضِرِ فِي الْمَطَرِ أَنْ يَجْمَعَ بَيْنَهُمَا فِي وَقْتِ الْأُولَى مِنْهُمَا.

12 "Close" is within 144 meters or 472 feet.

Travelers are entitled to combine:

1. the Noon and Midafternoon Prayers, during either of the two times one chooses; and
2. the Sunset and Night Prayers, during either of the two times one chooses.

Residents are entitled to combine the two [sets of prayers] during the time of the first of them when there is rain.

2.7 *Friday Prayer*

2.7.1 Conditions Obligating the Friday Prayer

(فَصْلٌ) وَشَرَائِطُ وُجُوبِ الْجُمُعَةِ سَبْعَةُ أَشْيَاءَ: الْإِسْلَامُ، وَالْبُلُوغُ، وَالْعَقْلُ، وَالْحُرِّيَّةُ، وَالذُّكُورَةُ، وَالصِّحَّةُ، وَالِاسْتِيطَانُ.

There are seven conditions that cause the Friday Prayer to be obligatory. [When the individual is:]

a. a Muslim;
b. mature;
c. of sound mind;
d. free;
e. male;
f. of sound health; and
g. a resident.

2.7.2 Conditions for Performance

وَشَرَائِطُ فِعْلِهَا ثَلَاثَةٌ: أَنْ تَكُونَ الْبَلَدُ مِصْرًا أَوْ قَرْيَةً، وَأَنْ يَكُونَ الْعَدَدُ أَرْبَعِينَ مِنْ أَهْلِ الْجُمُعَةِ، وَأَنْ يَكُونَ الْوَقْتُ بَاقِيًا؛ فَإِنْ خَرَجَ الْوَقْتُ أَوْ عُدِمَتِ الشُّرُوطُ صُلِّيَتْ ظُهْرًا.

The conditions for its performance are:

a. the location be a city or town;
b. the congregation numbers [at least] forty of those who are required to attend; and
c. its time remains.

If the time exits or one of the conditions ceases to exist, the Noon Prayer is performed.

2.7.3 Obligatory Elements

وَفَرَائِضُهَا ثَلَاثَةٌ: خُطْبَتَانِ يَقُومَ فِيهِمَا وَيَجْلِسَ بَيْنَهُمَا، وَأَنْ تُصَلَّى رَكْعَتَيْنِ فِي جَمَاعَةٍ.

The Friday Prayer has three obligatory elements:

a. two sermons: the imam stands while giving the two sermons and sits in between;
b. praying two *rak'at*; and
c. doing [the above] in a congregation.

2.7.4 Lesser Recommended Actions

وَهَيْئَاتُهَا أَرْبَعُ خِصالٍ: الْغُسْلُ، وَتَنْظِيفُ الْجَسَدِ، وَلُبْسُ الثِّيَابِ الْبِيْضِ، وَأَخْذُ الظُّفْرِ، وَالطِّيبُ. وَيُسْتَحَبُّ الْإِنْصَاتُ فِي وَقْتِ الْخُطْبَةِ، وَمَنْ دَخَلَ وَالْإِمَامُ يَخْطُبُ صَلَّى رَكْعَتَيْنِ خَفِيفَتَيْنِ ثُمَّ يَجْلِسُ.

It has four lesser recommended actions [*hay'āt*]. [One should:]

1. perform the purificatory bath and clean the body;
2. wear white;
3. trim one's nails; and
4. apply perfume.

It is recommended that one listen attentively during the sermon, and that anyone who enters [the mosque] during the imam's sermon prays two brief *rak'at* and then sits.

2.8 *The Two 'Eids*

(فَصْلٌ) وَصَلَاةُ الْعِيدَيْنِ سُنَّةٌ مُؤَكَّدَةٌ. وَهِيَ رَكْعَتَانِ: يُكَبِّرُ فِي الْأُولَى سَبْعًا سِوَى تَكْبِيرَةِ الْإِحْرَامِ، وَفِي الثَّانِيَةِ خَمْسًا سِوَى تَكْبِيرَةِ الْقِيَامِ. وَيَخْطُبُ بَعْدَهُمَا خُطْبَتَيْنِ: وَيُكَبِّرُ فِي الْأُولَى تِسْعًا وَفِي الثَّانِيَةِ سَبْعًا.

وَيُكَبِّرُ مِنْ غُرُوبِ الشَّمْسِ مِنْ لَيْلَةِ الْعِيدِ إِلَى أَنْ يَدْخُلَ الْإِمَامُ فِي الصَّلَاةِ، وَفِي الْأَضْحَى خَلْفَ الصَّلَوَاتِ الْمَفْرُوضَاتِ مِنْ صُبْحِ يَوْمِ عَرَفَةَ إِلَى الْعَصْرِ مِنْ آخِرِ أَيَّامِ التَّشْرِيقِ.

The 'Eid Prayer is an emphasized sunnah.

The 'Eid Prayer consists of two *rak'at*. In the first, the imam says *Allāhu akbar* seven times in addition to the opening *Allāhu akbar*; in the second, he says it five times in addition to the one for rising [from prostration].

The imam gives two sermons after the prayer. He says *Allāhu akbar* nine times during the first sermon and seven times during the second.

[One] says the customary litanies [*takbīr*] starting at the sunset preceding each 'Eid, continuing until the imam commences the 'Eid Prayer. During 'Eid al-'Aḍḥā one says this after the obligatory prayers, beginning on the Day of 'Arafah and continuing until after the Midafternoon Prayer on the last of the Days of Tashrīq [13 Dhi al-Ḥijjah].

2.9 *The Eclipse Prayer*

(فَصْلٌ) وَصَلَاةُ الْكُسُوفِ سُنَّةٌ مُؤَكَّدَةٌ، فَإِنْ فَاتَتْ لَمْ تُقْضَ. وَيُصَلِّي لِكُسُوفِ الشَّمْسِ وَخُسُوفِ الْقَمَرِ رَكْعَتَيْنِ، فِي كُلِّ رَكْعَةٍ قِيَامَانِ يُطِيلُ الْقِرَاءَةَ فِيهِمَا، وَرُكُوعَانِ يُطِيلُ التَّسْبِيحَ فِيهِمَا دُونَ السُّجُودِ، وَيَخْطُبُ بَعْدَهَا خُطْبَتَيْنِ. وَيُسِرُّ فِي كُسُوفِ الشَّمْسِ، وَيَجْهَرُ فِي خُسُوفِ الْقَمَرِ.

The Eclipse Prayer is an emphasized sunnah. It is not made up if missed.

Two *rak'at* are prayed during solar and lunar eclipses. Each *rak'ah* contains two standings wherein [the imam] lengthens the recitation, and two bowings wherein saying *subḥān Allah* is prolonged—though it is not prolonged during prostration.[13]

The imam gives two sermons after the prayer.

The prayer for the solar eclipse is silent, while the one for the lunar eclipse is audible.

2.10 *The Drought Prayer*

(فَصْلٌ) وَصَلَاةُ الِاسْتِسْقَاءِ مَسْنُونَةٌ. فَيَأْمُرُهُمُ الْإِمَامُ بِالتَّوْبَةِ وَالصَّدَقَةِ، وَالْخُرُوجِ مِنَ الْمَظَالِمِ، وَمُصَالَحَةِ الْأَعْدَاءِ، وَصِيَامِ ثَلَاثَةِ أَيَّامٍ. ثُمَّ يَخْرُجُ بِهِمُ الْإِمَامُ فِي الرَّابِعِ فِي ثِيَابِ بِذْلَةٍ وَاسْتِكَانَةٍ وَتَضَرُّعٍ، وَيُصَلِّي بِهِمْ رَكْعَتَيْنِ كَصَلَاةِ الْعِيدَيْنِ. ثُمَّ يَخْطُبُ بَعْدَهُمَا وَيُحَوِّلُ رِدَاءَهُ، وَيُكْثِرُ مِنَ الدُّعَاءِ وَالِاسْتِغْفَارِ، وَيَدْعُو بِدُعَاءِ رَسُولِ اللهِ - صَلَّى اللهُ عَلَيْهِ وَسَلَّمَ - وهو: «اللَّهُمَّ اجْعَلْها سُقْيَا رَحْمَةٍ وَلا تَجْعَلْها سُقْيَا عَذَابٍ وَلا مَحْقٍ وَلا بَلاءٍ، وَلا هَدْمٍ وَلا غَرَقٍ. اللَّهُمَّ عَلَى الظِّرَابِ وَالآكَامِ وَمَنَابِتِ الشَّجَرِ

13 The sound opinion is that one does prolong prostration similarly to prolonging bowing.

وَبُطُونِ الأَودِيَةِ. اللَّهُمَّ حَوَالَيْنَا وَلاَ عَلَيْنَا. اللَّهُمَّ اسْقِنَا غَيْثًا مغيثًا هَنِيئًا مَرِيئًا مَرِيعًا سَحًّا عامًّا غَدَقًا طَبَقاً مُجَلَّلًا دائمًا إلى يَوْمِ الدِّينِ. اللَّهُمَّ اسْقِنَا الغَيْثَ وَلا تَجْعَلْنَا مِنَ القَانِطِينَ. اللَّهُمَّ إِنَّ بِالعِبادِ وَالبِلاَدِ مِنَ الجَهْدِ وَالجُوْعِ وَالضَّنْكِ ما لا نَشْكُو إلاّ إِلَيْكَ. اللَّهُمَّ أَنْبِتْ لَنَا الزَّرْعَ وَأَدِرَّ لَنَا الضَّرْعَ وَأَنْزِلْ عَلَيْنَا مِنْ بَرَكَاتِ السَّمَاءِ وَأَنْبِتْ لَنَا مِنْ بَرَكَاتِ الأَرْضِ، وَاكْشِفْ عَنّا مِنَ البَلاءِ مَا لاَ يَكْشِفُهُ غَيْرُكَ. اللَّهُمَّ إِنَّا نَسْتَغْفِرُكَ إِنَّكَ كُنْتَ غَفَّارًا فَأَرْسِلِ السَّمَاءَ عَلَيْنَا مِدْرَارًا». وَيَغْتَسِلُ فِي الْوَادِي إِذَا سَالَ. وَيُسَبِّحُ لِلرَّعْدِ وَالْبَرْقِ.

The Drought Prayer is recommended. The imam orders the people to repent, give charity, cease being oppressive, seek reconciliation with enemies and fast three days. Then the imam goes out with them on the fourth day; they wear their work clothes, and are quiet and humble. He prays two *rak'at* with them, similar to the 'Eid Prayer. After the two *rak'at* he delivers a sermon and reverses his cloak. He makes much supplication and asks for forgiveness. He makes the supplication of the Prophet ﷺ, which is:

> O Allah, make it a water of mercy and do not make it a shower of torture, or wrath, trial, destruction or drowning.
>
> O Allah, upon the hills and bluffs, the thickets and valley floors.
>
> O Allah, around us, not upon us.
>
> O Allah, send us rain, raining wholesomely, healthily, torrentially, wide-spread, pouringly, in sheets, drenchingly, continuously until Judgment Day.
>
> O Allah, give us rain and make us not of those who despair.

> O Allah, servants and cities are in distress, hunger and want, from which we can ask none but You for relief.
>
> O Allah, make the crops grow and the milk of the livestock flow, and send down the blessings of the sky upon us and bring forth for us the blessings of the earth. Raise from us the affliction that none but You can lift.
>
> O Allah, we seek forgiveness from You since You are Oft-Forgiving, so let loose the sky upon us in torrents.

Those who attend the prayer wash in the valley if it flows, and say *subḥān Allah* for thunder and lightning.

2.11 *Prayer During Peril*

(فَصْلٌ) وَصَلَاةُ الْخَوْفِ عَلَى ثَلَاثَةِ أَضْرُبٍ.

أَحَدُهَا: أَنْ يَكُونَ الْعَدُوُّ فِي غَيْرِ جِهَةِ الْقِبْلَةِ، فَيُفَرِّقُهُمْ الْإِمَامُ فِرْقَتَيْنِ: فِرْقَةً تَقِفُ فِي وَجْهِ الْعَدُوِّ، وَفِرْقَةً خَلْفَهُ، فَيُصَلِّي بِالْفِرْقَةِ الَّتِي خَلْفَهُ رَكْعَةً ثُمَّ تُتِمُّ لِنَفْسِهَا وَتَمْضِي إِلَى وَجْهِ الْعَدُوِّ، وَتَأْتِي الطَّائِفَةُ الْأُخْرَى فَيُصَلِّي بِهَا رَكْعَةً وَتُتِمُّ لِنَفْسِهَا ثُمَّ يُسَلِّمُ بِهَا.

وَالثَّانِي: أَنْ يَكُونَ فِي جِهَةِ الْقِبْلَةِ، فَيَصُفُّهُمُ الْإِمَامُ صَفَّيْنِ وَيُحْرِمُ بِهِمْ، فَإِذَا سَجَدَ سَجَدَ مَعَهُ أَحَدُ الصَّفَّيْنِ وَوَقَفَ الصَّفُّ الْآخَرُ يَحْرُسُهُمْ، فَإِذَا رَفَعَ سَجَدُوا وَلَحِقُوهُ.

وَالثَّالِثُ: أَنْ يَكُونَ فِي شِدَّةِ الْخَوْفِ وَالْتِحَامِ الْحَرْبِ، فَيُصَلِّي كَيْفَ أَمْكَنَهُ، رَاجِلًا أَوْ رَاكِبًا مُسْتَقْبِلَ الْقِبْلَةِ وَغَيْرَ مُسْتَقْبِلٍ لَهَا.

There are three forms of prayer during peril.

The first form occurs when the enemy is not [located] in the direction of prayer. The imam divides the troops into two groups: one group stands facing the enemy while the other stands behind him. He prays one *rak'ah* with the group that is behind him, and [he prolongs his prayer while] the followers finish on their own and then head to face the enemy. The other group comes and he prays one *rak'ah* with them; they continue on their own [while he sits in *tashahhud*], waiting and he ends the prayer with them.

The second form occurs when the enemy is located in the direction of prayer. The imam arranges the followers in two lines and begins prayer with them. When he prostrates, one of the rows prostrates with him while the other row remains standing, guarding them; when he rises, the row that remained standing prostrates and catches up to him.

The third form occurs in the midst of peril and combat. One prays however one can: walking or riding; facing the direction of prayer or turned away.

2.12 *Clothes*

(فَصْلٌ) وَيُحَرَّمُ عَلَى الرِّجَالِ لُبْسُ الْحَرِيرِ وَالتَّخَتُّمُ بِالذَّهَبِ، وَيَحِلُّ لِلنِّسَاءِ، وَقَلِيلُ الذَّهَبِ وَكَثِيرُهُ فِي التَّحْرِيمِ سَوَاءٌ. وَإِذَا كَانَ بَعْضُ الثَّوْبِ إِبْرِيسَمًا وَبَعْضُهُ قُطْنًا أَوْ كَتَّانًا جَازَ لُبْسُهُ مَا لَمْ يَكُنْ الْإِبْرَيْسَمُ غَالِبًا.

It is unlawful for men to wear silk or gold [in general, even a] ring, though both are permissible for women. Small and large amounts of gold are identical with respect to impermissibility. If a portion of a garment is silk and another portion is cotton or linen, it is permissible [for men] to wear it as long as the silk [content] is not more than half.

3

FUNERALS

كِتَابُ الجَنَائِزِ

3.1 *Obligations Concerning the Deceased*

(فَصْلٌ) وَيَلْزَمُ فِي المَيِّتِ أَرْبَعَةُ أَشْيَاءَ: غُسْلُهُ، وَتَكْفِينُهُ، وَالصَّلَاةُ عَلَيْهِ، وَدَفْنُهُ. وَاثْنَانِ لَا يُغَسَّلَانِ وَلَا يُصَلَّى عَلَيْهِمَا: الشَّهِيدُ فِي مَعْرَكَةِ المُشْرِكِينَ، و السَّقْطُ الَّذِي لَمْ يَسْتَهِلَّ صَارِخًا.

Four things are required [to be done] for the deceased:

a. washing;
b. shrouding;
c. performing the Funeral Prayer; and
d. burial.

Two who are not washed or prayed over:

1. someone martyred while battling the polytheists; and
2. a fetus that did not show signs of life.

3.2 *Washing the Deceased*

وَيُغَسَّلُ المَيِّتُ وِتْرًا وَيَكُونُ فِي أَوَّلِ غُسْلِهِ سِدْرٌ، وَفِي آخِرِهِ شَيْءٌ مِنْ كَافُورٍ.

The deceased is washed an odd number of times. Lote tree is used in the first washing, and a bit of camphor in the last.

3.3 *The Shroud*

وَيُكَفَّنُ فِي ثَلَاثَةِ أَثْوَابٍ بِيضٍ لَيْسَ فِيهَا قَمِيصٌ وَلَا عِمَامَةٌ.

The deceased is shrouded in three white garments which do not include a long shirt or turban.

3.4 *The Funeral Prayer*

وَ يُكَبِّرُ عَلَيْهِ أَرْبَعَ تَكْبِيرَاتٍ يَقْرَأُ الْفَاتِحَةَ بَعْدَ الْأُولَى، وَيُصَلِّي عَلَى النَّبِيِّ – صَلَّى اللهُ عَلَيْهِ وَسَلَّمَ – بَعْدَ الثَّانِيَةِ. وَيَدْعُو لِلْمَيِّتِ بَعْدِ الثَّالِثَةِ، فَيَقُولُ: «اللَّهُمَّ هَذَا عَبْدُكَ وَابْنُ عَبْدَيْكَ، خَرَجَ مِنْ رَوْحِ الدُّنْيَا وَسَعَتِهَا وَمَحْبُوبِهِ وَأَحِبَّائِهِ فِيهَا إِلَى ظُلْمَةِ الْقَبْرِ وَمَا هُوَ لَاقِيهِ، كَانَ يَشْهَدُ أَنْ لَا إِلَهَ إِلَّا أَنْتَ وَحْدَكَ لَا شَرِيكَ لَكَ وَأَنَّ مُحَمَّدًا عَبْدُكَ وَرَسُولُكَ، وَأَنْتَ أَعْلَمُ بِهِ مِنَّا. اللَّهُمَّ إِنَّهُ نَزَلَ بِكَ وَأَنْتَ خَيْرُ مَنْزُولٍ بِهِ وَأَصْبَحَ فَقِيرًا إِلَى رَحْمَتِكَ وَأَنْتَ غَنِيٌّ عَنْ عَذَابِهِ وَقَدْ جِئْنَاكَ رَاغِبِينَ إِلَيْكَ شُفَعَاءَ لَهُ. اللَّهُمَّ إِنْ كَانَ مُحْسِنًا فَزِدْ فِي إِحْسَانِهِ وَإِنْ كَانَ مُسِيئًا فَتَجَاوَزْ عَنْهُ وَلَقِّهِ بِرَحْمَتِكَ رِضَاكَ، وَقِهِ فِتْنَةَ الْقَبْرِ وَعَذَابَهُ، وَافْسَحْ لَهُ فِي قَبْرِهِ، وَجَافِ الْأَرْضَ عَنْ جَنْبَيْهِ، وَلَقِّهِ بِرَحْمَتِكَ الْأَمْنَ مِنْ عَذَابِكَ حَتَّى تَبْعَثَهُ آمِنًا إِلَى جَنَّتِكَ بِرَحْمَتِكَ يَا أَرْحَمَ الرَّاحِمِينَ». وَيَقُولُ فِي الرَّابِعَةِ: «اللَّهُمَّ لَا تَحْرِمْنَا أَجْرَهُ وَلَا تَفْتِنَّا بَعْدَهُ وَاغْفِرْ لَنَا وَلَهُ». وَيُسَلِّمُ بَعْدَ الرَّابِعَةِ.

[During the prayer,] *Allāhu akbar* is said over the deceased four times. After saying it the first time, one reads *al-Fātiḥa*. After the second, one recites prayers over the Prophet ﷺ. After the third, one supplicates for the deceased saying:

> O Allah, this is Your servant, son of two of Your servants. He has left the comfort of this world and its abundance and the things he loved and the people who loved him, on to the darkness of the grave and what waits ahead. He testified that there is no deity

> except You—You only, without partner—and that Muḥammad is Your slave and messenger. And You are more knowledgeable of him than we are.
>
> O Allah, verily he has gone to remain with You and You are the best with whom one could remain. He has become in need of Your mercy, while You have no need to torture him. We have come to You, seeking for him Your intercession.
>
> O Allah, if he was good then increase him in his goodness; if he was wicked then forgive him and meet him with Your mercy and Your satisfaction [with him]. Protect him from the trial of the grave and its torture. Make his grave spacious for him, and spread the ground away from his flanks. And through Your mercy, meet him with amnesty from Your torture until You resurrect him to his paradise in safety, by Your mercy, O most merciful of the merciful!

During the fourth, one says:

> O Allah, do not deprive us of his reward, nor afflict us after him. [O Allah,] grant us and him forgiveness.

After the fourth, one says *al-salāmu ʿalaykum.*

3.5 *Burial*

وَيُدْفَنُ فِي لَحْدٍ مُسْتَقْبِلَ الْقِبْلَةِ، وَيُسَلُّ مِنْ قِبَلِ رَأْسِهِ بِرِفْقٍ وَيَقُولُ الَّذِي يَلْحَدُهُ: «بِاسْمِ اللَّهِ وَعَلَى مِلَّةِ رَسُولِ اللَّهِ» - صَلَّى اللهُ عَلَيْهِ وَسَلَّمَ. وَيُضْجَعُ فِي الْقَبْرِ بَعْدَ أَنْ يُعَمَّقَ قَامَةً وَبَسْطَةً. وَيُسَطَّحُ القَبْرُ وَلَا يُبْنَى عَلَيْهِ، وَلَا يُجَصَّصُ.

The deceased is buried in a trench grave [*laḥd*] facing the direction of prayer. He is lowered gently into the grave, head-first, from the direction where his feet will rest. The person who places him in the grave should say:

> *Bismillāh, wa 'alā millati rasūli llāh* (In the name of Allah, and according to the religion of the Messenger of Allah ﷺ).

The deceased should be placed in the grave on his [right] side, after the grave has been dug deep enough that one can stand and extend his arms [without his fingertips extending beyond the grave].

The grave is made level [with the surrounding ground]. It should not be built upon or covered with gypsum.

وَلَا بَأْسَ بِالْبُكَاءِ عَلَى الْمَيِّتِ مِنْ غَيْرِ نَوْحٍ وَلَا شَقِّ جَيْبٍ. وَيُعَزَّى أَهْلُهُ إِلَى ثَلَاثَةِ أَيَّامٍ مِنْ دَفْنِهِ. وَلَا يُدْفَنُ اثْنَانِ فِي قَبْرٍ وَاحِدٍ إِلَّا لِحَاجَةٍ.

There is no harm in crying over the deceased provided one does not wail or rip one's collar.

Condolences are given to the family of the deceased for up to three days after his burial.

Two [individuals] are not buried in a single grave except out of necessity.

4

ZAKĀH

كِتَابُ الزَّكَاةِ

4.1 *Properties on Which Zakāh is Obligatory*

تَجِبُ الزَّكَاةُ فِي خَمْسَةِ أَشْيَاءَ، وَهِيَ: المَوَاشِي، وَالْأَثْمَانُ، وَالزُّرُوعُ، وَالثِّمَارُ، وَعُرُوضُ التِّجَارَةِ.

Zakāh is obligatory on five types of property:

1. livestock;
2. money;
3. agriculture;
4. fruit; and
5. trade goods.

4.1.1 Livestock

فَأَمَّا المَوَاشِي فَتَجِبُ الزَّكَاةُ فِي ثَلَاثَةِ أَجْنَاسٍ مِنْهَا، وَهِيَ: الْإِبِلُ، وَالْبَقَرُ، وَالْغَنَمُ. وَشَرَائِطُ وُجُوبِهَا سِتَّةُ أَشْيَاءَ: الْإِسْلَامُ، وَالْحُرِّيَّةُ، وَالمِلْكُ التَّامُّ، وَالنِّصَابُ، وَالْحَوْلُ، وَالسَّوْمُ.

Zakāh is obligatory on three types of livestock:

1. camels;
2. cows; and
3. sheep [and goats].

It is obligatory when six conditions are met. [That the owner:]

a. is a Muslim;
b. is free;
c. possesses complete ownership;[1]
d. possesses the minimum amount [*niṣāb*];
e. year; and
f. that the animals are grazed [on herbage that grows without human intervention].

4.1.2 Money

وَأَمَّا الْأَثْمَانُ فَشَيْئَانِ: الذَّهَبُ وَالْفِضَّةُ. وَشَرَائِطُ وُجُوبِ الزَّكَاةِ فِيهَا خَمْسَةُ أَشْيَاءَ: الْإِسْلَامُ، وَالْحُرِّيَّةُ، وَالْمِلْكُ التَّامُّ، وَالنِّصَابُ، وَالْحَوْلُ.

[Zakāh is obligatory] on two types of money:[2]

1. gold; and
2. silver.

It is obligatory when five conditions are met. [The owner must:]

a. be a Muslim;
b. be free;
c. possess complete ownership;
d. possess the minimal amount; and
e. year.

1 This agrees with the old Shafi'i school. However, this is not a condition according to the new school.

2 Other instruments that take the place of gold and silver are subject to zakāh as trade goods. Following this, the *fulūs* token-money of the past was not subject to zakāh as gold and silver, but rather as trade goods. See al-Jāwī, et al, *Qūt al-Ḥabib al-Gharib*, 99.

4.1.3 Agriculture

وَأَمَّا الزُّرُوعُ فَتَجِبُ الزَّكَاةُ فِيهَا بِثَلَاثَةِ شَرَائِطَ: أَنْ يَكُونَ مِمَّا يَزْرَعُهُ الْآدَمِيُّونَ، وَأَنْ يَكُونَ قُوتًا مُدَّخَرًا، وَأَنْ يَكُونَ نِصَابًا وَهُوَ خَمْسَةُ أَوْسُقٍ لَا قِشْرَ عَلَيْهَا.

Zakāh from agriculture is obligatory when [the crops fulfill] three conditions. The crops must be:

a. sown by humans;
b. staple food crops; and
c. the minimum amount: 5 *awsuq* [609.84 kg or 1344.5 lbs], devoid of the [outer] husk [or shell].

4.1.4 Fruit

وَأَمَّا الثِّمَارُ فَتَجِبُ الزَّكَاةُ فِي شَيْئَيْنِ مِنْهَا: ثَمَرَةُ النَّخْلِ، وَثَمَرَةُ الْكَرْمِ. وَشَرَائِطُ وُجُوبِ الزكاة فيهَا أَرْبَعَةُ أَشْيَاءَ: الْإِسْلَامُ، وَالْحُرِّيَّةُ، وَالْمِلْكُ التَّامُّ، وَالنِّصَابُ.

Zakāh is obligatory on two types of fruits:

1. dates; and
2. grapes.

Zakāh is obligatory on [fruits] when four conditions are met. [The owner must:]

a. be a Muslim;
b. be free;
c. have complete ownership; and
d. possess the minimum amount.

4.1.5 Trade Goods

وَأَمَّا عُرُوضُ التِّجَارَةِ فَتَجِبُ الزَّكَاةُ فِيهَا بِالشَّرَائِطِ الْمَذْكُورَةِ فِي الْأَثْمَانِ.

Zakāh is obligatory on trade goods according to the conditions mentioned for money.

4.2 *Camels*

(فَصْلٌ) وَأَوَّلُ نِصَابِ الْإِبِلِ خَمْسٌ وَفِيهَا شَاةٌ، وَفِي عَشْرٍ شَاتَانِ، وَفِي خَمْسَ عَشْرَةَ ثَلَاثُ شِيَاهٍ، وَفِي عِشْرِينَ أَرْبَعُ شِيَاهٍ، وَفِي خَمْسٍ وَعِشْرِينَ بِنْتُ مَخَاضٍ، وَفِي سِتٍّ وَثَلَاثِينَ بِنْتُ لَبُونٍ، وَفِي سِتٍّ وَأَرْبَعِينَ حِقَّةٌ، وَفِي إِحْدَى وَسِتِّينَ جَذَعَةٌ، وَفِي سِتٍّ وَسَبْعِينَ بِنْتَا لَبُونٍ، وَفِي إِحْدَى وَتِسْعِينَ حِقَّتَانِ، وَفِي مِائَةٍ وَإِحْدَى وَعِشْرِينَ ثَلَاثُ بَنَاتِ لَبُونٍ. ثُمَّ فِي كُلِّ أَرْبَعِينَ بِنْتُ لَبُونٍ، وَفِي كُلِّ خَمْسِينَ حِقَّةٌ.

The minimum number of camels is 5, on which [the obligatory zakāh] is 1 *shāh*.[3] On 10 camels, there are two *shāh*; on 15, three *shāh*; on 20, four. On 25 camels, there is one *bint makhāḍ*; on 36, one *bint labūn*; on 46, one *ḥiqqah*; on 61, one *jadh'ah*; 76, two *bint labūn*; 91, two *ḥiqqah*; and 121, three *bint labūn*.[4]

From thereon, for every 40 there is one *bint labūn* and for every 50, one *ḥiqqah*.[5]

4.3 *Cows*

(فَصْلٌ) وَأَوَّلُ نِصَابِ الْبَقَرِ ثَلَاثُونَ وَفِيهَا تَبِيعٌ، وَفِي كُلِّ أَرْبَعِينَ مُسِنَّةٌ، وَعَلَى هَذَا أَبَدًا فَقِسْ.

---

3 The word *shāh* applies to both a one-year-old sheep (*shāh jadha'ah*) and a two-year-old goat (*thaniyyah*).

4 A *bint makhāḍ* is a one-year-old female camel; a *bint labūn* is a two-year-old female camel; an *ibn labūn* is a two-year-old male camel; a *ḥiqqah* is a three-year-old female camel; and a *jadh'ah* is a four-year-old female camel.

5 So, for 140 camels, 2 *ḥiqqah* and 1 *bint labūn* are owed; for 150 camels, 3 *ḥiqqah* are owed; and for 200 camels, either 4 *ḥiqqah* or 5 *bint labūn* are owed.

The minimum number of cows is 30, on which [the obligatory zakāh] is one *tabī‘*; on 40, there is one *musinnah*.[6]

Other cases are calculated similarly.[7]

4.4   *Sheep and Goats*

(فَصْلٌ) وَأَوَّلُ نِصَابِ الْغَنَمِ أَرْبَعُونَ وَفِيهَا شَاةٌ جَذَعَةٌ مِنْ الضَّأْنِ أَوْ ثَنِيَّةٌ مِنْ الْمَعَزِ، وَفِي مِائَةٍ وَإِحْدَى وَعِشْرِينَ شَاتَانِ، وَفِي مِائَتَيْنِ وَوَاحِدَةٍ ثَلَاثُ شِيَاهٍ، [وَفِي أَرْبَعِمِائَةٍ أَرْبَعُ شِيَاهٍ،] ثُمَّ فِي كُلِّ مِائَةٍ شَاةٌ.

The minimum number of sheep and goats is 40, on which [the obligatory zakāh] is one *shāh jadha‘ah* sheep or one *thaniyyah* goat; on 121, there are two *shāh*; on 201, three; on 400, four. After that, on every [multiple of] 100, one *shāh*.[8]

4.5   *Conditions for Mixed Flocks*

(فَصْلٌ) والْخَلِيطانِ يُزَكِّيَانِ زَكَاةَ الْوَاحِدِ بِسَبْعَةِ شَرَائِطَ: إِذَا كَانَ الْمُرَاحُ وَاحِدًا، وَالْمُسْرَحُ وَاحِدًا، وَالْمُرْعَى وَاحِدًا، وَالْفَحْلُ وَاحِدًا، وَالْمُشْرَبُ وَاحِدًا، وَالْحَالِبُ وَاحِدًا، وَمَوْضِعُ الْحَلْبِ وَاحِدًا.

Mixed flocks extract the zakāh of a single flock provided seven conditions are met:

a.   the livestock bed in the same place at night;
b.   they gather in the same place before being taken to drink;
c.   the pasture is the same;
d.   the stud is the same;

---

6   A *tabī‘* is a one-year-old cow; a *musinnah* is a two-year-old cow.
7   So, for 120 cows, 3 *musinnah* or 4 *tabī‘* are owed.
8   So, for 500 sheep, 5 *shāh* are owed.

e. what they drink is the same;
f. they are milked by the same person;[9] and
g. the place of milking is the same.

4.6 *Gold and Silver*

(فَصْلٌ) وَنِصَابُ الذَّهَبِ عِشْرُونَ مِثْقَالًا، وَفِيهِ رُبُعُ الْعُشْرِ وَهُوَ نِصْفُ مِثْقَالٍ، وفِيمَا زَادَ بِحِسَابِهِ. وَنِصَابُ الْوَرِقِ مِائَتَا دِرْهَمٍ، وَفِيه رُبُعُ الْعُشْرِ، وَهُوَ خَمْسَةُ دَرَاهِمَ، وَفِيمَا زَادَ بِحِسَابِهِ. وَلَا تَجِبُ فِي الْحُلِيِّ الْمُبَاحِ زَكَاةٌ.

The minimum amount for gold is 20 *mithqāl* [85 grams or 2.73 troy ounces], on which there is [a zakāh of] 2.5% (a half *mithqāl*); anything above this is calculated according to the same proportion.

The minimum amount for silver is 200 *dirham* [595 grams or 19.13 troy ounces], on which there is [a zakāh of] 2.5% (five *dirham*) and anything above this is calculated according to the same proportion.

Zakāh is not obligatory on lawful jewelry.

4.7 *Agriculture and Fruit*

(فَصْلٌ) وَنِصَابُ الزُّرُوعِ وَالثِّمَارِ خَمْسَةُ أَوْسُقٍ، وَهِيَ أَلْفٌ وَسِتُّمِائَةِ رِطْلٍ بِالْعِرَاقِيِّ، وَفِيمَا زَادَ بِحِسَابِهِ. وَفِيهَا إِنْ سُقِيَتْ بِمَاءِ السَّمَاءِ أَوْ السَّيْحِ الْعُشْرُ، وَإِنْ سُقِيَتْ بِدُولَابٍ أَوْ بِنَضْحٍ نِصْفُ الْعُشْرِ.

The minimum amount for agriculture and fruit is 5 *awsuq* (1600 Iraqi *riṭl*) [609.84 kg or 1344.5 lbs] and anything additional is

9 The strongest opinion is that this is not a requirement.

calculated according to this proportion.

A zakāh of 10% is owed if the crop was irrigated through rain or flooding. If it was irrigated by buckets or by conveying water from one place to another, then it is half [i.e., 5%].

4.8 *Trade Goods*

(فَصْلٌ) وَتُقَوَّمُ عُرُوضُ التِّجَارَةِ عِنْدَ الْحَوْلِ بِمَا اشْتُرِيَتْ بِهِ، وَيُخْرَجُ مِنْ ذَلِكَ رُبُعُ الْعُشْرِ. وَمَا اسْتُخْرِجَ مِنْ مَعَادِنِ الذَّهَبِ وَالْفِضَةِ يُخْرَجُ مِنْهُ رُبُعَ الْعُشْرِ فِي الْحَالِ. وَمَا يُوجَدُ مِنَ الرِّكَازِ فَفِيهِ الْخُمُسُ.

The value of trade goods is appraised at the end of the year based on the currency with which the goods were purchased; [a zakāh of] 2.5% is taken from its value.

[A zakāh of] 2.5% is taken from gold and silver ore immediately [after separating the ore from the dirt].

[A zakāh of] 20% is taken from [gold and silver] treasure.

4.9 *Zakāt al-Fiṭr*

(فَصْلٌ) وَتَجِبُ زَكَاةُ الْفِطْرِ بِثَلَاثَةِ شَرَائِطَ: الْإِسْلَامُ، وَبِغُرُوبِ الشَّمْسِ مِنْ آخِرِ يَوْمٍ مِنْ شَهْرِ رَمَضَانَ، وَوُجُودُ الْفَضْلِ عَنْ قُوتِهِ وَقُوتِ عِيَالِهِ فِي ذَلِكَ الْيَوْمِ.

وَيُزَكِّي عَنْ نَفْسِهِ وَعَمَّنْ تَلْزَمُهُ نَفَقَتُهُ مِنَ الْمُسْلِمِينَ صَاعًا مِنْ قُوتِ بَلَدِهِ، وقَدْرُهُ خَمْسَةُ أَرْطَالٍ وَثُلُثٌ بِالْعِرَاقِيِّ.

Zakāt al-Fiṭr is obligatory when three [conditions are met]:

a. the person is a Muslim;

b. the sun has set on the last day of Ramadan; and
c. on that day [the person paying it] has provisions in excess of the his own needs and the needs of his dependents.

One gives zakāh for oneself and all Muslims one is required to support. [The amount is] one *ṣa'* [2.03 liters] of the stored staple foods of the region; its amount equals 5 1/3 Iraqi *riṭl*.

4.10 *Distributing Zakāh*

(فَصْلٌ) وَتُدْفَعُ الزَّكَاةُ إِلَى الْأَصْنَافِ الثَّمَانِيَةِ الَّذِينَ ذَكَرَهُمُ اللهُ تَعَالَى فِي كِتَابِهِ الْعَزِيزِ فِي قَوْلِهِ تَعَالَى: «إِنَّمَا الصَّدَقَاتُ لِلْفُقَرَاءِ وَالْمَسَاكِيْنِ وَالْعَامِلِيْنَ عَلَيْهَا وَالْمُؤَلَّفَةِ قُلُوبُهُمْ وَفِي الرِّقَابِ وَالْغَارِمِينَ وَفِي سَبِيْلِ اللهِ وَابْنِ السَّبِيْلِ» وإِلَى مَنْ يُوجَدُ مِنْهُمْ وَلَمْ يُجْزِ الِاقْتِصَارُ عَلَى أَقَلَّ مِنْ ثَلَاثَةٍ مِنْ كُلِّ صِنْفٍ إِلَّا الْعَامِلَ.

Zakāh is given to the eight categories that Allah Most High mentioned in His mighty book, where He Most High said:

> *The alms are only for the poor and the needy, and those who collect them, and those whose hearts are to be reconciled, and to free the captives and the debtors, and for the cause of Allah, and (for) the wayfarers...*[10]

One does not give to less than three recipients from each category when they exist—except for zakāh workers.

4.10.1 Impermissible Recipients

وَخَمْسَةٌ لَا يَجُوزُ دَفْعُهَا إِلَيْهِمْ: الْغَنِيُّ بِمَالٍ أَوْ كَسْبٍ، وَالْعَبْدُ، وَبَنُو هَاشِمٍ، وَبَنُو الْمُطَّلِبِ، وَالْكَافِرُ. وَمَنْ تَلْزَمُ الْمُزَكِّيَ نَفَقَتُهُ لَا يَدْفَعُهَا إِلَيْهِمْ بِاسْمِ الْفُقَرَاءِ وَالْمَسَاكِيْنِ.

---

10 Qur'ān, 9:60,

It is not permissible to give zakāh to five types of people:

1. someone who is self-sufficient due to wealth or work;
2. slaves;
3. descendants of Banī Hāshim or Banī al-Muṭṭalib;
4. non-Muslims; and
5. whoever the zakāh giver is required to support: zakāh is not given to them under the category of the poor and impoverished.[11]

11 According to the most obvious reading, the pronoun "them" is limited to this final category. See al-Jāwī, et al, *Qūt al-Ḥabib al-Gharīb,* 112; al-Bayjūrī, et al, Ḥāshiyat al-Bayjūrī, 1:106; and al-Sharbīnī, et al, *Al-Iqnā',* 249.

5

FASTING

كِتَابُ الصِّيَامِ

5.1 *Conditions Obligating the Fast*

وَشَرَائِطُ وُجُوبِ الصِّيَامِ أَرْبَعَةُ أَشْيَاءَ: الْإِسْلَامُ، وَالْبُلُوغُ، وَالْعَقْلُ، وَالْقُدْرَةُ عَلَى الصَّوْمِ.

Fasting [the month of Ramadan] is obligatory when four conditions are met. [When the person is:]

a. a Muslim;
b. mature;
c. of sound mind; and
d. able to fast.

5.2 *Obligatory Actions*

وَفَرَائِضُ الصَّوْمِ أَرْبَعَةُ أَشْيَاءَ: النِّيَّةُ، وَالْإِمْسَاكُ عَنْ الْأَكْلِ وَالشُّرْبِ وَالْجِمَاعِ، وَتَعَمُّدِ الْقَيْءِ.

There are four obligatory actions of fasting:

a. intention; and
b–d. abstaining from: eating and drinking, intercourse and inducing vomit.

5.3 *Things that Invalidate the Fast*

وَالَّذِي يُفْطِرُ بِهِ الصَّائِمُ عَشَرَةُ أَشْيَاءَ: مَا وَصَلَ عَمْدًا إِلَى الْجَوْفِ وَالرَّأْسِ، والْحُقْنَةُ فِي أَحَدِ السَّبِيلَيْنِ، وَالْقَيْءُ عَمْدًا، وَالْوَطْءُ عَمْدًا فِي الْفَرْجِ، وَالإِنْزَالُ عَنْ مُبَاشَرَةٍ، وَالْحَيْضُ، وَالنِّفَاسُ، وَالْجُنُونُ، وَالرِّدَّةُ.

The fast is invalidated if any of the following ten things occur:

1. anything intentionally reaching a [body] cavity [including the brain, chest and abdomen], or the head, through an orifice;[1]
3. insertion of something into the anus, urethra or vagina;
4. intentional vomiting;
5. intentional intercourse;
6. ejaculation resulting from skin contact;
7. menstruation;
8. postnatal bleeding;
9. insanity; and
10. apostasy [May Allah protect us!].

5.4 *Recommended Actions*

وَيُسْتَحَبُّ فِي الصَّوْمِ ثَلَاثَةُ أَشْيَاءَ: تَعْجِيلُ الْفِطْرِ، وَتَأْخِيرُ السَّحُورِ، وَتَرْكُ الْهُجْرِ مِنَ الْكَلَامِ.

وَيَحْرُمُ صِيَامُ خَمْسَةِ أَيَّامٍ: الْعِيدَانِ، وَأَيَّامُ التَّشْرِيقِ الثَّلَاثَةُ. وَيُكْرَهُ صَوْمُ يَوْمِ الشَّكِّ إِلَّا أَنْ يُوَافِقَ عَادَةً لَهُ.

There are three recommended actions of fasting. [One should:]

---

1 This applies to substances introduced to the body through the openings of the mouth, nostrils, ears and genitals. It does not apply to substances introduced through the eyes or absorbed through the skin.

1. hasten to break the fast;
2. delay the [pre-dawn] meal prior to fasting; and
3. avoid repulsive speech.

It is unlawful to fast on five days:

1. the two 'Eids;
2. the three Days of Tashrīq [the three days immediately after 'Eid al-Aḍḥā].

It is offensive to fast the Day of Doubt [*yaum al-shakk*], unless fasting it coincides with an individual's habitual fast.[2]

5.5 *Making Up and Expiations*

وَمَنْ وَطِئَ فِي نَهَارِ رَمَضَانَ عَامِدًا فِي الْفَرْجِ فَعَلَيْهِ الْقَضَاءُ وَالْكَفَّارَةُ وَهِيَ عِتْقُ رَقَبَةٍ مُؤْمِنَةٍ، فَإِنْ لَمْ يَجِدْ فَصِيَامُ شَهْرَيْنِ مُتَتَابِعَيْنِ، فَإِنْ لَمْ يَسْتَطِعْ فَإِطْعَامُ سِتِّينَ مِسْكِينًا لِكُلِّ مِسْكِينٍ مُدٌّ.

وَمَنْ مَاتَ وَعَلَيْهِ صِيَامٌ مِنْ رَمَضَانَ أُطْعِمَ عَنْهُ لِكُلِّ يَوْمٍ مُدٌّ. وَالشَّيْخُ إِنْ عَجَزَ عَنِ الصَّوْمِ يُفْطِرُ وَيُطْعِمُ عَنْ كُلِّ يَوْمٍ مُدًّا. وَالْحَامِلُ وَالْمُرْضِعُ إِذَا خَافَتَا عَلَى أَنْفُسِهِمَا أَفْطَرَتَا وَعَلَيْهِمَا الْقَضَاءُ، فَإِنْ خَافَتَا عَلَى أَوْلَادِهِمَا أَفْطَرَتَا وَعَلَيْهِمَا الْقَضَاءُ وَالْكَفَّارَةُ عَنْ كُلِّ يَوْمٍ مُدٌّ، وَهُوَ رِطْلٌ وَثُلُثٌ بِالْعِرَاقِيِّ. وَالْمَرِيضُ وَالْمُسَافِرُ سَفَرًا طَوِيلًا يُفْطِرَانِ وَيَقْضِيَانِ.

Anyone who has intentional vaginal intercourse in the daytime during Ramadan must make up the fast-day and perform an ex-

2 The Day of Doubt is the 30th of Sha'bān when the previous night was cloudy and no one reported sighting the new moon; *or* people speak about it being seen but the witnesses do not meet the necessary conditions for giving testimony.

piation. The expiation is emancipating a Muslim slave. If a slave is not found, one fasts consecutively for two months. If one is unable to do this, he feeds 60 of the poor, giving each one *mudd* [0.51 liters] of food.

If someone dies while still owing fast-days from Ramadan, one *mudd* [0.51 liters] of food for each fast-day missed is given on his behalf.

Someone who is elderly and unable to fast gives one *mudd* [0.51 liters] of food for each fast-day missed.

When a woman who is pregnant or nursing fears for herself, she breaks her fast and must make up the fast-day. If she fears for the child [only], she must make up the fast-day *and* offer an expiation for each day missed. The expiation is one *mudd*.[3]

Someone who is ill or making a long journey is not required to fast, but must make up the fast-days.

5.6 *Spiritual Retreat*

(فَصْلٌ) وَالِاعْتِكَافُ سُنَّةٌ مُستَحَبَّةٌ. وَلَهُ شَرْطَانِ: النِّيَّةُ، واللُّبْثُ فِي المَسْجِدِ. وَلَا يَخْرُجُ مِنَ الِاعْتِكَافِ المَنْذُورِ إِلَّا لِحَاجَةِ الْإِنْسَانِ، أَوْ عُذْرٍ مِنْ حَيْضٍ، أَوْ مَرَضٍ لَا يُمْكِنُ المُقَامُ مَعَهُ. وَيَبْطُلُ بِالوَطْءِ.

Spiritual retreat [*i'tikāf*] is a recommended sunnah. It has two conditions. [One must:]

a. make intention; and
b. remain in the mosque.

3 The expiation is given to the poor and impoverished, but not to the other recipients of zakāh.

One does not prematurely exit a spiritual retreat one has vowed to make except for the sake of human need [e.g., going to the lavatory], or an excuse (such as menstruation or sickness) which prevents one from remaining in the mosque.

Intercourse invalidates a spiritual retreat.

6

PILGRIMAGE

كِتَابُ الْحَجِّ

6.1 *Conditions Obligating Hajj*

وَشَرَائِطُ وُجُوبِ الْحَجِّ سَبْعَةُ أَشْيَاءَ: الْإِسْلَامُ، وَالْبُلُوغُ، وَالْعَقْلُ، وَالْحُرِّيَّةُ، وَوُجُودُ الزَّادِ وَالرَّاحِلَةِ، وَتَخْلِيَةُ الطَّرِيقِ، وَإِمْكَانُ الْمَسِيرِ.

There are seven conditions obligating Ḥajj. [One must:]

a. be Muslim;
b. be mature;
c. be sane;
d. be free;
e. possess excess provisions and a means of transportation;
f. have safe passage; and
g. be able to travel.

6.2 *Integrals of Ḥajj*

وَأَرْكَانُ الْحَجِّ أَرْبَعَةٌ: الْإِحْرَامُ مَعَ النِّيَّةِ، وَالْوُقُوفُ بِعَرَفَةَ، وَالطَّوَافُ، وَالسَّعْيُ بَيْنَ الصَّفَا وَالْمَرْوَةِ.

There are four integrals of Ḥajj. [One must:]

a. enter the state of *iḥrām* accompanied by intention;
b. stand on [the plain of] ʿArafah;

c. circumambulate the House [seven times]; and
d. traverse between Ṣafā and Marwā [seven times].[1]

6.3 *Integrals of ʿUmrah*

وَأَرْكَانُ الْعُمْرَةِ أَرْبَعَةٌ: الْإِحْرَامُ، وَالطَّوَافُ، وَالسَّعْيُ، وَالْحَلْقُ أَوِ التَّقْصِيرُ فِي أَحَدِ الْقَوْلَيْنِ.

There are four integrals of ʿUmrah. [One must:]

a. enter the state of *iḥrām* [with intention];
b. circumambulate the House;
c. traverse [between Ṣafā and Marwā]; and
d. shave or trim the hair (according to one of two opinions).[2]

6.4 *Obligatory Actions of Ḥajj*

وَوَاجِبَاتُ الْحَجِّ غَيْرُ الْأَرْكَانِ ثَلَاثَةُ أَشْيَاءَ: الْإِحْرَامُ مِنَ الْمِيقَاتِ، وَرَمْيُ الْجِمَارِ الثَّلَاثِ، وَالْحَلْقُ.

There are three obligatory actions during Ḥajj other than the integrals. [One must:]

a. enter *iḥrām* at the proper place and time [*mīqāt*];
b. throw stones at the three pillars; and
c. shave the head.[3]

---

1 According to the most reliable opinion, shaving or trimming the hair is a fifth integral.
2 The opinion listed in the book is the preponderant opinion.
3 This is an integral, not obligatory.

6.5 *Recommended Actions*

وَسُنَنُ الْحَجِّ سَبْعٌ: الْإِفْرَادُ وَهُوَ تَقْدِيمُ الْحَجِّ عَلَى الْعُمْرَةِ، وَالتَّلْبِيَةُ، وَطَوَافُ الْقُدُومِ، وَالْمَبِيتُ بِمُزْدَلِفَةَ، وَرَكْعَتَا الطَّوَافِ، وَالْمَبِيتُ بِمِنًى، وَطَوَافُ الْوَدَاعِ.

وَيَتَجَرَّدُ الرَّجُلُ عِنْدَ الْإِحْرَامِ عَنِ الْمَخِيطِ وَيَلْبَسُ إِزَارًا وَرِدَاءً أَبْيَضَيْنِ.

Seven actions are recommended during Ḥajj. [One should:]

1. perform Ḥajj before ‘Umrah [*ifrād*];
2. say *labayk Allah ummma labayk…*;
3. perform the Arrival Circumambulation;
4. stay the night at Muzdalifah;
5. perform the two-*rak‘at* Circumambulation Prayer;
6. stay the night at Minā; and
7. perform the Farewell Circumambulation.[4]

Men divest themselves of stitched garments upon entering *iḥrām*, and wear a white waist-wrapper and mantle.[5]

6.6 *Things Unlawful During Ḥajj*

(فَصْلٌ) وَيَحْرُمُ عَلَى الْمُحْرِمِ عَشَرَةُ أَشْيَاءَ: لُبْسُ الْمَخِيطِ، وَتَغْطِيَةُ الرَّأْسِ مِنَ الرَّجُلِ وَالْوَجْهِ وَالْكَفَّيْنِ مِنَ الْمَرْأَةِ، وَتَرْجِيلُ الشَّعْرِ وَحَلْقُهُ، وَتَقْلِيمُ الْأَظْفَارِ، وَالطِّيبُ، وَقَتْلُ الصَّيْدِ، وَعَقْدُ النِّكَاحِ، وَالْوَطْءُ، وَالْمُبَاشَرَةُ بِشَهْوَةٍ. وَفِي جَمِيعِ ذَلِكَ الْفِدْيَةُ إِلَّا عَقْدَ النِّكَاحِ فَإِنَّهُ لَا يَنْعَقِدُ. وَلَا يُفْسِدُهُ إِلَّا الْوَطْءُ فِي الْفَرْجِ، وَلَا يَخْرُجُ مِنْهُ بِالْفَسَادِ.

---

4 According to stronger opinions, numbers four, six, and seven are all considered obligatory.

5 It is obligatory to do these things, however that the waist-wrapper and mandle are white is recommmended.

Ten things are unlawful to a person in the state of *iḥrām*. [One must not:]

1. wear stitched garments [if male];
2. cover the head if male, or the face if female;
3–4. apply oil to or remove hair;[6]
5. pare one's nails;
6. use perfume;
7. kill a game animal;
8. contract a marriage;
9. have intercourse; nor
10. engage in sexual foreplay.

There is an expiation [*fidyah*] for each of the above, except for contracting a marriage—which [simply] is not valid.

None of the above invalidate Ḥajj except for intercourse. Invalidating Ḥajj does not release one from the state of *iḥrām*.

6.7 *Omissions During Ḥajj*

وَمَنْ فَاتَهُ الْوُقُوفُ بِعَرَفَةَ تَحَلَّلَ بِعَمَلِ عُمْرَةٍ وَعَلَيْهِ الْقَضَاءُ وَالْهَدْيُ. وَمَنْ تَرَكَ رُكْنًا لَمْ يَحِلَّ مِنْ إِحْرَامِهِ حَتَّى يَأْتِيَ بِهِ.

وَمَنْ تَرَكَ وَاجِبًا لَزِمَهُ دَمٌ. وَمَنْ تَرَكَ سُنَّةً لَمْ يَلْزَمْهُ بِتَرْكِهَا شَيْءٌ.

Someone who omits:

1. *standing on 'Arafah*: is released from performing Ḥajj by performing 'Umrah [instead]. Such a person must perform a make-up Ḥajj and slaughter a *hady*.

---

6 Combing the hair, applying oil to it, and scratching it are all offensive since they can lead to removing hair. Shaving and all forms of hair removal are unlawful.

2. *an integral*: is not released from his *iḥrām* until he performs it.
3. *an obligatory action*: must offer a sacrifice.
4. *a recommended action*: is not required to do anything on account of its omission.

6.8 *Expiation*

(فَصْلٌ) وَالدِّمَاءُ الْوَاجِبَةُ فِي الْإِحْرَامِ خَمْسَةُ أَشْيَاءَ:

أَحَدُهَا: الدَّمُ الْوَاجِبُ بِتَرْكِ نُسُكٍ، وَهُوَ عَلَى التَّرْتِيبِ: شَاةٌ، فَإِنْ لَمْ يَجِدْ فَصِيَامُ عَشَرَةِ أَيَّامٍ: ثَلَاثَةٍ فِي الْحَجِّ وَسَبْعَةٍ إِذَا رَجَعَ إِلَى أَهْلِهِ.

وَالثَّانِي: الدَّمُ الْوَاجِبُ بِالْحَلْقِ وَالتَّرَفُّهِ، وَهُوَ عَلَى التَّخْيِيرِ: شَاةٌ، أَوْ صَوْمُ ثَلَاثَةِ أَيَّامٍ، أَوِ التَّصَدُّقُ بِثَلَاثَةِ آصُعٍ عَلَى سِتَّةِ مَسَاكِينَ.

وَالثَّالِثُ: الدَّمُ الْوَاجِبُ بِالْإِحْصَارِ فَيَتَحَلَّلُ وَيُهْدِي شَاةً.

وَالرَّابِعُ: الدَّمُ الْوَاجِبُ بِقَتْلِ الصَّيْدِ وَهُوَ عَلَى التَّخْيِيرِ: إِنْ كَانَ الصَّيْدُ مِمَّا لَهُ مِثْلٌ أَخْرَجَ الْمِثْلَ مِنْ النَّعَمِ، أَوْ قَوَّمَهُ وَاشْتَرَى بِقِيمَتِهِ طَعَامًا وَتَصَدَّقَ بِهِ، أَوْ صَامَ عَنْ كُلِّ مُدٍّ يَوْمًا. وَإِنْ كَانَ الصَّيْدُ مِمَّا لَا مِثْلَ لَهُ أَخْرَجَ بِقِيمَتِهِ طَعَامًا أَوْ صَامَ عَنْ كُلِّ مُدٍّ يَوْمًا.

وَالْخَامِسُ: الدَّمُ الْوَاجِبُ بِالْوَطْءِ وَهُوَ عَلَى التَّرْتِيبِ: بَدَنَةٌ، فَإِنْ لَمْ يَجِدْهَا فَبَقَرَةٌ، فَإِنْ لَمْ يَجِدْهَا فَسَبْعٌ مِنَ الْغَنَمِ، فَإِنْ لَمْ يَجِدْهَا قَوَّمَ الْبَدَنَةَ وَاشْتَرَى بِقِيمَتِهَا طَعَامًا وَتَصَدَّقَ بِهِ، فَإِنْ لَمْ يَجِدْهَا صَامَ عَنْ كُلِّ مُدٍّ يَوْمًا.

وَلَا يُجْزِئُهُ الْهَدْيُ وَلَا الْإِطْعَامُ إِلَّا بِالْحَرَمِ، وَيُجْزِئُهُ أَنْ يَصُومَ حَيْثُ شَاءَ.

وَلَا يَجُوزُ قَتْلُ صَيْدِ الْحَرَمِ وَلَا قَطْعُ شَجَرِهِ، وَالْمُحِلُّ وَالْمُحْرِمُ فِي ذَلِكَ سَوَاءٌ.

There are five types of obligatory blood sacrifice during Ḥajj:

a. *For omitting one of the* [*obligatory, non-integral*] *rites*: it is according to [the following] order:[7]
   1. a *shah*;
   2. if one is not found, then fasting ten days: three during Ḥajj and seven when one returns to one's family;
b. *For shaving and* [*use of*] *luxuries*:[8] one must choose one of the following:
   1. a *shah*;
   2. fasting three days; or
   3. giving three *ṣā'* [of food; 6.09 liters] in charity, distributed among six of the poor.
c. *For being held back* [*from completion*]: one is released from Ḥajj and required to sacrifice one *shāh*.
d. *For killing a game animal*:
   1. If there exists a game animal similar [to the one killed], then one has the choice of:
      i. giving a camel, cow, goat or sheep [when it is] analogous; or
      ii. appraising its value and buying food of the same value that is given as charity; or
      iii. fasting one day for each *mudd* [0.51 liters] [of food that the amount would have purchased].
   2. If a similar game animal does not exist, then one:
      i. gives its value in charity; or
      ii. fasts one day for each *mudd* [0.51 liters] of food [that the amount would have purchased].
e. *For intercourse*: it is according to [the following] order [and

7 The preponderant opinion is that the correct order is to slaughter a sheep and donate its meat to the poor in the vicinity of the Sacred Precint, to donate its value in food, or—lacking the ability to do either of the first two —to fast.

8 Luxuries include using perfume and applying oil to the hair.

only the male must make the expiation]:

1. a male or female camel.
2. If one cannot be found, one gives a cow.
3. If one cannot be found, one gives seven sheep or goats.
4. If sheep cannot be found, then the value of a camel suitable for sacrifice[9] is appraised and one uses the value to buy food which one gives in charity.
5. If one does not find this, then one fasts one day for each 0.51 liters of food [the amount would have purchased].

Giving food and performing a[n expiatory] sacrifice suffice only when given in the Sacred Precinct. It suffices to fast wherever one wishes.

It is not permissible to kill game within the Sacred Precinct, nor to cut its trees. This [ruling] is the same whether or not one is in the state of *iḥrām*.

9 See "13.3 Offering Sacrifices" on page 141.

7

SELLING AND OTHER TRANSACTIONS

كِتَابُ الْبُيُوعِ وَغَيْرِهَا مِنَ الْمُعَامَلَاتِ

7.1 *Types of Sales*

الْبُيُوعُ ثَلَاثَةُ أَشْيَاءَ: بَيْعُ عَيْنٍ مُشَاهَدَةٍ فَجَائِزٌ، وَبَيْعُ شَيْءٍ مَوْصُوفٍ فِي الذِّمَّةِ فَجَائِزٌ إِذَا وُجِدَتْ الصِّفَةُ عَلَى مَا وُصِفَتْ بِهِ، وَبَيْعُ عَيْنٍ غَائِبَةٍ لَمْ تُشَاهَدْ فَلَا يَجُوزُ.

وَيَصِحُّ بَيْعُ كُلِّ طَاهِرٍ مُنْتَفَعٍ بِهِ مَمْلُوكٍ، وَلَا يَصِحُّ بَيْعُ عَيْنٍ نَجِسَةٍ وَلَا بَيْعُ مَا لَا مَنْفَعَةَ فِيهِ.

Selling is three types of transactions.

1. Selling an item that is seen first hand: it is permissible.[1]
2. Selling something based on guaranteed attributes: it is permissible if the item's attributes are found to be as described.
3. Selling an item that is not present and not seen first hand: it is not permissible.

It is permissible to sell all items that are:

a. pure;
b. useful; and
c. fully-owned.

---

1 When the word "permissible" is associated with contracts, it indicates validity. When it is associated with actions, it indicates lawfulness.

It is not valid to sell an item that is:

a. filthy; or
b. useless.

7.2 *Unlawful Gain* [*ribā*]

(فَصْلٌ) وَالرِّبَا فِي الذَّهَبِ وَالْفِضَّةِ وَالْمَطْعُومَاتِ. وَلَا يَجُوزُ بَيْعُ الذَّهَبِ بِالذَّهَبِ وَلَا الْفِضَّةِ كَذَلِكَ إِلَّا مُتَمَاثِلًا نَقْدًا، وَلَا بَيْعُ مَا ابْتَاعَهُ حَتَّى يَقْبِضَهُ، وَلَا بَيْعُ اللَّحْمِ بِالْحَيَوَانِ.

وَيَجُوزُ بَيْعُ الذَّهَبِ بِالْفِضَّةِ مُتَفَاضِلًا نَقْدًا، وَكَذَلِكَ الْمَطْعُومَاتُ لَا يَجُوزُ بَيْعُ الْجِنْسِ مِنْهَا بِمِثْلِهِ إِلَّا مُتَمَاثِلًا نَقْدًا، وَيَجُوزُ بَيْعُ الْجِنْسِ مِنْهَا بِغَيْرِهِ مُتَفَاضِلًا نَقْدًا، وَلَا يَجُوزُ بَيْعُ الْغَرَرِ.

[Transactions involving] gold, silver and foodstuffs may incur unlawful gain [*ribā*].

It is not permissible to buy gold for gold, nor silver for silver, unless the quantities are equal and it is paid for on the spot [*naqdan*].

It is not permissible to sell something one has purchased until taking possession of it.

It is not permissible to sell meat for a [live] animal.

It is permissible to buy gold for silver where the quantities differ, as long as it is paid for on the spot.

It is the same with foodstuffs: it is not permissible to sell something of the same type and kind, unless it is for the same quantity and paid for on the spot.

It is permissible to sell foodstuffs of one type and quality for another quality where there is a difference in quantity, as long as it is paid for on the spot.

It is not to permissible to engage in transactions based on risk.

7.3 *Choosing to Rescind*

(فَصْلٌ) وَالْمُتَبَايِعَانِ بِالْخِيَارِ مَا لَمْ يَتَفَرَّقَا، وَلَهُمَا أَنْ يَشْرِطَا الْخِيَارَ لَهُمَا إِلَى ثَلَاثَةِ أَيَّامٍ. وَإِذَا وُجِدَ بِالْمَبِيعِ عَيْبٌ فَلِلْمُشْتَرِي رَدُّهُ.

The transactors are entitled to choose [to rescind the sale] as long as they have not parted company.

They are both entitled to stipulate to rescind the sale for up to three days.

If the sold item is found to be defective,[2] the buyer is entitled to return it.

7.4 *Impermissible Transactions*

وَلَا يَجُوزُ بَيْعُ الثَّمَرَةِ مُطْلَقًا إِلَّا بَعْدَ بُدُوِّ صَلَاحِهَا. وَلَا بَيْعُ مَا فِيهِ الرِّبَا بِجِنْسِهِ رَطْبًا إِلَّا اللَّبَنَ.

It is not permissible to sell fruit unconditionally, except after ripeness becomes apparent.[3]

2 An item is defective when it has a flaw that reduces the item's value or hinders an intended use, and the item is typically free of such a flaw.

3 It is permissible to sell unripe fruit still on the tree if its immediate harvest is stipulated.

It is not permissible to sell something wherein unlawful gain exists[4] when it contains liquid, except for dairy products [e.g., milk, yogurt, buttermilk, and sour milk].

7.5 *Ordering Goods*

(فَصْلٌ) وَيَصِحُّ السَّلَمُ حَالًّا وَمُؤَجَّلًا فِيمَا تَكَامَلَ فِيهِ خَمْسَةُ شَرَائِطَ: أَنْ يَكُونَ مَضْبُوطًا بِالصِّفَةِ، وَأَنْ يَكُونَ جِنْسًا لَمْ يَخْتَلِطْ بِهِ غَيْرُهُ، وَلَمْ تَدْخُلْهُ النَّارُ لِإِحَالَتِهِ، وَلَا يَكُونَ مُعَيَّنًا، وَلَا مِنْ مُعَيَّنٍ.

ثُمَّ لِصِحَّةِ الْمُسْلَمِ فِيهِ ثَمَانِيَةُ شَرَائِطَ، وهي: أَنْ يَصِفَهُ بَعْدَ ذِكْرِ جِنْسِهِ وَنَوْعِهِ بِالصِّفَاتِ الَّتِي يَخْتَلِفُ بِهَا الثَّمَنُ، وَأَنْ يَذْكُرَ قَدْرَهُ بِمَا يَنْفِي الْجَهَالَةَ عَنْهُ، وَإِنْ كَانَ مُؤَجَّلًا ذُكِرَ وَقْتُ مَحِلِّهِ، وَأَنْ يَكُونَ مَوْجُودًا عِنْدَ الِاسْتِحْقَاقِ فِي الْغَالِبِ، وَأَنْ يُذْكَرَ مَوْضِعُ قَبْضِهِ، وَأَنْ يَتَقَابَضَا قَبْلَ التَّفَرُّقِ، وَأَنْ يَكُونَ عَقْدُ السَّلَمِ نَاجِزًا لَا يَدْخُلُهُ خِيَارُ الشَّرْطِ.

It is permissible to order goods [*salam*], [deliverable] immediately or deferred, provided the goods fulfill five conditions:

a. its attributes are defined;
b. it is a single type, not mixed with others;
c. it is not transformed by artificial heat;
d. it is not a specific item; nor
e. from something specific.

After that, the goods bought must meet the following eight conditions in order for the transaction to be valid:

---

4 This is when one is selling it for an item of the same type.

a. once its type and kind have been mentioned, the attributes that change its price are described;
b. its measure [i.e., dimensions, weight, etc.] is mentioned in a way that removes all ignorance;
c. if [the delivery] is deferred, the due date is mentioned;
d. the goods are usually available at the time the transaction becomes due;
e. the place of delivery is mentioned;
f. the price is known;
g. the deal becomes final [and the capital is paid] before the transactors part company; and
h. the deal is final, without any stipulation to rescind.

7.6 *Offering Collateral*

(فَصْلٌ) وَكُلُّ مَا جَازَ بَيْعُهُ جَازَ رَهْنُهُ فِي الدُّيُونِ إِذَا اسْتَقَرَّ ثُبُوتُهَا فِي الذِّمَّةِ، وَلِلرَّاهِنِ الرُّجُوعُ فِيهِ مَا لَمْ يَقْبِضْهُ. وَلَا يَضْمَنُهُ الْمُرْتَهِنُ إِلَّا بِالتَّعَدِّي، وَإِذَا قَضَى بَعْضَ الْحَقِّ لَمْ يَخْرُجْ شَيْءٌ مِنْ الرَّهْنِ حَتَّى يَقْضِيَ جَمِيعَهُ.

Anything that can be sold can be offered as collateral for loans once the loan has become irrevocably established as a personal debt. The one offering collateral may void the transaction as long as the other party has not taken possession of the item.

The one holding the collateral is not liable for damages except for transgression [*al-ta'addi*]. If he takes possession of some of what is due, none of the collateral is released until all of the debt is settled.

7.7 *Suspension*

(فَصْلٌ) وَالْحَجْرُ عَلَى سِتَّةٍ: الصَّبِيُّ، وَالْمَجْنُونُ، وَالسَّفِيهُ الْمُبَذِّرُ لِمَالِهِ، وَالْمُفْلِسُ الَّذِي ارْتَكَبَتْهُ الدُّيُونُ، وَالْمَرِيضُ فِيمَا زَادَ عَلَى الثُّلُثِ، وَالْعَبْدُ الَّذِي لَمْ يُؤْذَنْ لَهُ فِي التِّجَارَةِ.

وَتَصَرُّفُ الصَّبِيِّ وَالْمَجْنُونِ وَالسَّفِيهِ غَيْرُ صَحِيحٍ، وَتَصَرُّفُ الْمُفْلِسِ يَصِحُّ فِي ذِمَّتِهِ دُونَ أَعْيَانِ مَالِهِ، وَتَصَرُّفُ المَرِيضِ فِيمَا زَادَ عَلَى الثُّلُثِ مَوْقُوفٌ عَلَى إِجَازَةِ الْوَرَثَةِ مِنْ بَعْدِهِ، وَتَصَرُّفُ الْعَبْدِ يَكُونُ فِي ذِمَّتِهِ يُتْبَعُ بِهِ بَعْدَ عِتْقِهِ.

Six [types of] people are suspended from transactions. [One who is:]

1. still a minor;
2. insane;
3. a spendthrift;
4. insolvent;
5. [terminally] ill and close to death: in any transaction exceeding one-third of their estate; and
6. a slave who has not been given permission to engage in trade.

The transactions of a minor, someone insane or a spendthrift are invalid.

The transactions of a spendthrift are valid as personal debt, but not against his personal effects [including money].

The transactions of someone ill or close to death in excess of one-third of the estate are suspended pending the heirs' consent after his death.

The transactions of a slave are his personal debt [*dhimma*] and follow him when he is freed.

7.8 *Reconciliation*

(فَصْلٌ) وَيَصِحُّ الصُّلْحُ مَعَ الْإِقْرَارِ فِي الْأَمْوَالِ الثَّابِتَةِ فِي الذِّمَّةِ وَمَا يُفْضِي إِلَيْهَا. وَهُوَ نَوْعَانِ: إِبْرَاءٌ، وَمُعَاوَضَةٌ. فَالْإِبْرَاءُ: اقْتِصَارُهُ مِنْ حَقِّهِ عَلَى بَعْضِهِ، وَلَا يَجُوزُ فِعْلُهُ عَلَى شَرْطٍ. وَالْمُعَاوَضَةُ: عُدُولُهُ عَنْ حَقِّهِ إِلَى غَيْرِهِ، وَيَجْرِي عَلَيْهِ حُكْمُ الْبَيْعِ.

Reconciliation is permissible when there is an admission[5] concerning property and what has the potential to convert into property.[6] Reconciliation is of two types:

1. *Absolution* [*ibrā'*]: it is reducing the debt; it is not permissible to make absolution contingent upon a condition.
2. *Compensation* [*mu'āwaḍa*]: it is accepting something else in place of what is owed. It is subject to the rulings concerning transactions.

7.8.1 Property Issues

وَيَجُوزُ لِلْإِنْسَانِ أَنْ يُشْرِعَ رَوْشَنًا فِي طَرِيقٍ نَافِذٍ بِحَيْثُ لَا يَتَضَرَّرُ الْمَارُّ بِهِ، وَلَا يَجُوزُ فِي الدَّرْبِ الْمُشْتَرَكِ إِلَّا بِإِذْنِ الشُّرَكَاءِ.

وَيَجُوزُ تَقْدِيمُ الْبَابِ فِي الدَّرْبِ الْمُشْتَرَكِ، وَلَا يَجُوزُ تَأْخِيرُهُ إِلَّا بِإِذْنٍ مِنَ الشُّرَكَاءِ.

It is permissible for a person to begin construction of a balcony [*rawshan*] over a non-dead-end alley, provided it does not hamper traffic. It is not permissible to do so over a dead-end alley, except with permission from those who share its usage.

It is permissible to move one's door closer to the beginning of a dead-end alley that is shared with others; it is not permissible to move it deeper into the alley without permission from the others who share the alley.

---

5 See "7.14 Admissions" on page 75.
6 An example of the latter includes claims for personal injuries.

7.9 *Assignment of Debt*

(فَصْلٌ) وَشَرَائِطُ الْحَوَالَةِ أَرْبَعَةُ أَشْيَاءَ: رِضَا الْمُحِيلِ، وَقَبُولُ الْمُحْتَالِ، وَكَوْنُ الْحَقِّ مُسْتَقِرًّا فِي الذِّمَّةِ، وَاتِّفَاقُ مَا فِي ذِمَّةِ الْمُحِيلِ وَالْمُحَالِ عَلَيْهِ فِي الْجِنْسِ وَالنَّوْعِ وَالْحُلُولِ وَالتَّأْجِيلِ. وَتَبْرَأُ بِهَا ذِمَّةُ الْمُحِيلِ.

[At the start of this transaction, we have A, B and C. A owes B, and B owes C. B removes himself by giving C the right to collect the debt A owes him. In such a scenario, A is the *muḥāl ʿalayhi*, B the *muḥīl*, and C the *muḥtāl*.] The conditions for assigning debt are four:

a. B's consent;
b. C's approval;
c. the amount owed has become [irrevocably] established; and
d. the amount owed by A and B agree in:
    1. type and kind, and
    2. being due now, or in the future [at the same time].

By doing this, B's debt [to C] becomes absolved [and A]'s debt to B becomes A's debt to C.

7.10 *Guaranteeing Payment*

(فَصْلٌ) وَيَصِحُّ ضَمَانُ الدُّيُونِ الْمُسْتَقَرَّةِ فِي الذِّمَّةِ إِذَا عُلِمَ قَدْرُهَا، وَلِصَاحِبِ الْحَقِّ مُطَالَبَةُ مَنْ شَاءَ مِنَ الضَّامِنِ وَالْمَضْمُونِ عَنْهُ إِذَا كَانَ الضَّمَانُ عَلَى مَا بَيَّنَّاهُ. وَإِذَا غَرِمَ الضَّامِنُ رَجَعَ عَلَى الْمَضْمُونِ عَنْهُ إِذَا كَانَ الضَّمَانُ وَالْقَضَاءُ بِإِذْنِهِ. وَلَا يَصِحُّ ضَمَانُ الْمَجْهُولِ، وَلَا مَا لَمْ يَجِبْ إِلَّا دَرْكَ الْمَبِيعِ.

It is permissible to guarantee payment of debts that have the potential to become irrevocably established, if the amount is known. The person owed is entitled to seek payment from the guarantor and the one for whom he guarantees, if the debt is as we have clarified. If the guarantor pays, he seeks reimbursement from the one for whom he guaranteed if the guarantee and payment was with his permission.

It is not permissible to guarantee something that is not specified or not yet due, except guaranteeing that a sale item is legitimate.

7.11 *Guaranteeing Physical Presence*

(فَصْلٌ) والكَفَالة بالبَدَنِ جَائِزَةٌ إِذَا كَانَ عَلَى المَكْفُولِ بِهِ حَقٌّ لِآدَمِيٍّ.

It is permissible to guarantee [another's] physical presence if the one whose presence is being guaranteed owes something to another person.[7]

7.12 *Partnerships*

(فَصْلٌ) وَلِلشَّرِكَةِ خَمْسُ شَرَائِطَ: أَنْ تَكُونَ عَلَى نَاضٍّ مِنَ الدَّرَاهِمِ وَالدَّنَانِيرِ، أَنْ يَتَّفِقَا فِي الْجِنْسِ وَالنَّوْعِ، وَأَنْ يَخْلِطَا المَالَيْنِ، وَأَنْ يَأْذَنَ كُلُّ وَاحِدٍ مِنْهُمَا لِصَاحِبِهِ فِي التَّصَرُّفِ، وَأَنْ يَكُونَ الرِّبْحُ وَالْخُسْرَانُ عَلَى قَدْرِ المَالَيْنِ.

وَلِكُلِّ وَاحِدٍ مِنْهُمَا فَسْخُهَا مَتَى شَاءَ، وَمَتَى مَاتَ أَحَدُهُمَا بَطَلَتْ.

There are five conditions for a partnership:

a. the capital is based on gold or silver currency;[8]
b. the capital agrees in type and quality;

7 This includes crimes such as murder and accusations of illicit sex; but not theft, drinking intoxicants and fornication. See "16.5 Rights" on page 154.

8 Stronger opinions within the school indicate that any form of capital is valid provided it meets the requirements for ordering goods. See al-Sharbīnī, et al, *Al-Iqnā'*, 332; al-Jāwī, et al, *Qūt al-Ḥabīb al-Gharīb*, 151; and al-Bayjūrī, et al, *Ḥāshiyat al-Bayjūrī*, 1:412.

c. the capital is mixed together;
d. each partner allows the other to engage in transactions; and
e. profit and loss are commensurate with each partner's contribution.

Each partner is entitled to dissolve the partnership at will.

If one of the partners dies, the partnership is void.

7.13 *Commissioning Others*

(فَصْلٌ) وَكُلُّ مَا جَازَ لِلْإِنْسَانِ التَّصَرُّفُ فِيهِ بِنَفْسِهِ جَازَ لَهُ أَنْ يُوَكِّلَ فِيهِ أَوْ يَتَوَكَّلَ.
والوَكَالَةُ عَقْدٌ جَائِزٌ، وَلِكُلِّ وَاحِدٍ مِنْهُمَا فَسْخُهَا مَتَى شَاءَ، وَتَنْفَسِخُ بِمَوْتِ أَحَدِهِمَا.

وَالْوَكِيلُ أَمِينٌ فِيمَا يَقْبِضُهُ وَفِيمَا يَصْرِفُهُ، وَلَا يَضْمَنُ إِلَّا بِالتَّفْرِيطِ. وَلَا يَجُوزُ أَنْ يَبِيعَ وَيَشْتَرِيَ إِلَّا بِثَلَاثَةِ شَرَائِطَ: أَنْ يَبِيعَ بِثَمَنِ الْمِثْلِ، وَأَنْ يَكُونَ بِنَقْدِ الْبَلَدِ. وَلَا يَجُوزُ أَنْ يَبِيعَ مِنْ نَفْسِهِ. وَلَا يُقِرَّ عَلَى مُوَكِّلِهِ إِلَّا بِإِذْنِهِ.

It is permissible to:

1. commission an agent to perform on one's behalf, and
2. be commissioned as an agent to perform on another's behalf,

any transaction that one is permitted to engage in.

The commission is a revocable contract: each party is entitled to rescind it at will. It is voided upon the death of either party.

The commissioned agent is considered reliable enough to take possession and engage in transactions. He is not liable for damages, except due to negligence.

It is not permissible [for the commissioned agent] to buy and sell except under three conditions. [The agent must:]

a. buy at the typical price;
b. purchase with immediate payment—not on credit; and
c. [that it be] the local currency.

The commissioned agent may not purchase from himself, nor make an admission against the one who appointed him [in arguing a claim] except with his permission.[9]

7.14 *Admissions*

(فَصْلٌ) وَالْمُقَرُّ بِهِ ضَرْبَانِ: حَقُّ اللهُ تَعَالَى، وَحَقُّ الْآدَمِيِّ. فَحَقُّ اللهِ تَعَالَى يَصِحُّ الرُّجُوعُ فِيهِ عَنْ الْإِقْرَارِ بِهِ. وَحَقُّ الْآدَمِيِّ لَا يَصِحُّ الرُّجُوعُ فِيهِ عَنْ الْإِقْرَارِ بِهِ.

Admissions concern two types [of rights]:

1. rights owed to Allah Most High, and
2. rights owed to human beings.[10]

It is valid to retract one's admission concerning rights owed Allah to Most High.

It is not valid to retract one's admission concerning rights owed to human beings.

---

9 It is not valid to do so, even with permission. See al-Bayjūrī, et al, *Ḥāshiyat al-Bayjūrī*, 1:418.
10 See "16.5 Rights" on page 154.

7.14.1 Conditions

وَتَفْتَقِرُ صِحَّةُ الْإِقْرَارِ إِلَى ثَلَاثَةِ شَرَائِطَ: الْبُلُوغُ، وَالْعَقْلُ، وَالِاخْتِيَارُ. وَإِنْ كَانَ بِمَالٍ
أُعْتُبِرَ فِيهِ شَرْطٌ رَابِعٌ، وَهُوَ: الرُّشْدُ. وَإِذَا أَقَرَّ بِمَجْهُولٍ رَجَعَ لَهُ فِي بَيَانِهِ. وَيَصِحُّ
الِاسْتِثْنَاءُ فِي الْإِقْرَارِ إِذَا وَصَلَهُ بِهِ. وَهُوَ فِي حَالِ الصِّحَّةِ وَالْمَرَضِ سَوَاءٌ.

Three [characteristics] are necessary in order for the admission to be valid. [The one making the admission must be:]

a. mature;
b. of sound mind; and
c. free from coercion.

If it concerns property, then a fourth condition is considered. [The one making the declaration must be:]

d. rational.

If one admits to something unspecified, he is asked for clarification.

It is valid to exclude things from the admission, provided the [phrase used for the] exclusion is connected [to the admission].

It is the same whether the person making the admission is in good health or sick.

7.15 *Lending*

(فَصْلٌ) وَكُلُّ مَا أَمْكَنَ الِانْتِفَاعُ بِهِ مَعَ بَقَاءِ عَيْنِهِ جَازَتْ إِعَارَتُهُ إِذَا كَانَتْ مَنَافِعُهُ
آثَارًا. وَتَجُوزُ الْعَارِيَّةُ مُطْلَقَةً وَمُقَيَّدَةً بِمُدَّةٍ، وَهِيَ مَضْمُونَةٌ عَلَى الْمُسْتَعِيرِ بِقِيمَتِهَا
يَوْمَ تَلَفِهَا.

It is permissible to lend anything that can be benefitted from as long as the item itself is not consumed, and as long as the benefit is a service.

It is permissible to lend something without restriction; it is [also] permissible to restrict its duration.

The borrower is liable for it. [The amount owed is] based on the value [not price] the day the item was destroyed [not the day it was lent].

7.16 *Wrongfully-Taken Property*

(فَصْلٌ) وَمَنْ غَصَبَ مَالًا لِأَحَدٍ لَزِمَهُ رَدُّهُ وَأَرْشُ نَقْصِهِ وَأُجْرَةُ مِثْلِهِ. فَإِنْ تَلِفَ ضَمِنَهُ بِمِثْلِهِ إِنْ كَانَ لَهُ مِثْلٌ، أَوْ بِقِيمَتِهِ إِنْ لَمْ يَكُنْ لَهُ مِثْلٌ أَكْثَرَ مَا كَانَتْ مِنْ يَوْمِ الْغَصْبِ إِلَى يَوْمِ التَّلَفِ.

Whoever wrongfully takes property is required to return the property with compensation for damages and its rental value [for the duration it was taken].

If the property is destroyed, one replaces it with an identical item if one exists. [Otherwise,] one is liable for its maximum value [not price] from the time it was taken until the day it was destroyed.

7.17 *Preemption*

(فَصْلٌ) وَالشُّفْعَةُ وَاجِبَةٌ بِالْخُلْطَةِ دُونَ الْجِوَارِ فِيمَا يَنْقَسِمُ دُونَ مَا لَا يَنْقَسِمُ وَفِي كُلِّ مَا لَا يُنْقَلُ مِنْ الْأَرْضِ وَغَيْرِهِ بِالثَّمَنِ الَّذِي وَقَعَ عَلَيْهِ الْبَيْعُ. وَهِيَ عَلَى الْفَوْرِ، فَإِنْ أَخَّرَهَا مَعَ الْقُدْرَةِ عَلَيْهَا بَطَلَتْ. وَإِذَا تَزَوَّجَ امْرَأَةً عَلَى شِقْصٍ أَخَذَهُ الشَّفِيعُ بِمَهْرِ الْمِثْلِ. وَإِنْ كَانَ الشُّفَعَاءُ جَمَاعَةً اسْتَحَقُّوهَا عَلَى قَدْرِ الْأَمْلَاكِ.

Preemption is an intrinsic right when:

a. there is joint ownership (but not in neighboring properties);
b. in things that retain their original utility when divided (not in things that do not);
c. in things that cannot be transported, such as real estate and others; and
d. for the agreed upon sale price.

Preemption must be declared immediately. It is void when one delays even though one is able to preempt.

If one marries a woman [and her agreed upon marriage payment is] a parcel of land that a co-owner preempts, the co-owner must pay her the amount similar women receive.

If preemption is opted for by a group, the entitlement of each is in proportion to their ownership.[11]

7.18 *Financing a Profit-Sharing Venture*

(فَصْلٌ) وَلِلْقِرَاضِ أَرْبَعَةُ شَرَائِطَ: أَنْ يَكُونَ عَلَى نَاضٍّ مِنَ الدَّرَاهِمِ وَالدَّنَانِيرِ، وَأَنْ يَأْذَنَ رَبُّ المَالِ لِلْعَامِلِ فِي التَّصَرُّفِ مُطْلَقًا أَوْ فِيمَا لَا يَنْقَطِعُ وُجُودُهُ غَالِبًا، وَأَنْ يَشْتَرِطَ لَهُ جُزْءًا مَعْلُومًا مِنَ الرِّبْحِ، وَأَنْ لَا يُقَدَّرَ بِمُدَّةٍ.

وَلَا ضَمَانَ عَلَى الْعَامِلِ إِلَّا بِعُدْوَانٍ. وَإِذَا حَصَلَ رِبْحٌ وَخُسْرَانٌ جُبِرَ الْخُسْرَانُ بِالرِّبْحِ.

Financing profit-sharing ventures is permissible under four conditions:

11 Given A, B, and C, where A owns 1/2, B 1/3, and C 1/6: if A sells and B and C preempt, B will end up with 2/3 of the total property, and C 1/3. Both before and after preemption, B owns twice that of C.

a. the contract is based on gold or silver currency;
b. the financier permits the worker to engage in trade that is unrestricted *or* restricted to things typically available;
c. the financier stipulates for the worker a known portion of the profit; and
d. the contract is not limited to a fixed duration.

The worker is not liable, except when there is transgression.

If there is both profit and loss, the loss is compensated by the profits.

7.19 *Watering Crops for a Stipulated Portion*

(فَصْلٌ) وَالْمُسَاقَاةُ جَائِزَةٌ عَلَى النَّخْلِ وَالْكَرْمِ. وَلَهَا شَرْطَانِ: أَحَدُهُمَا: أَنْ يُقَدِّرَهَا بِمُدَّةٍ مَعْلُومَةٍ. وَالثَّانِي: أَنْ يُعَيِّنَ لِلْعَامِلِ جُزْءًا مَعْلُومًا مِنَ الثَّمَرَةِ.

ثُمَّ الْعَمَلُ فِيهَا عَلَى ضَرْبَيْنِ: عَمَلٌ يَعُودُ نَفْعُهُ عَلَى الثَّمَرَةِ فَهُوَ عَلَى الْعَامِلِ، وَعَمَلٌ يَعُودُ نَفْعُهُ إِلَى الْأَرْضِ فَهُوَ عَلَى رَبِّ الْمَالِ.

Watering crops for a stipulated portion of the crops is valid for dates and grapes. It has two conditions:

a. the specification of a known duration; and
b. the specification of a known portion of the crops for the worker.

With respect to watering crops, work falls under two categories:

1. work, the benefit of which returns to the crops: it is required from the worker; and
2. work, the benefit of which returns to the land: it is required from the owner.

7.20 *Renting Goods and Hiring Services*

(فَصْلٌ) وَكُلُّ مَا أَمْكَنَ الِانْتِفَاعُ بِهِ مَعَ بَقَاءِ عَيْنِهِ صَحَّتْ إِجَارَتُهُ إِذَا قُدِّرَتْ مَنْفَعَتُهُ بِأَحَدِ أَمْرَيْنِ: مُدَّةٍ أَوْ عَمَلٍ. وَإِطْلَاقُهَا يَقْتَضِي تَعْجِيلَ الْأُجْرَةِ، إِلَّا أَنْ يُشْتَرَطَ التَّأْجِيلُ.

وَلَا تَبْطُلُ الْإِجَارَةُ بِمَوْتِ أَحَدِ الْمُتَعَاقِدَيْنِ، وَتَبْطُلُ بِتَلَفِ الْعَيْنِ الْمُسْتَأْجَرَةِ. وَلَا ضَمَانَ عَلَى الْأَجِيرِ إِلَّا بِعُدْوَانٍ.

It is permissible to rent items from which benefit is derived, provided the item is not consumed, and provided the benefit is specified by either:

1. duration; or
2. work to be performed.

Wages are due in advance unless they are stipulated to be deferred.

The contract is not nullified by the death of one of the parties.

It is voided if the rented item is destroyed.

The renter is not liable unless there is a transgression.

7.21 *Wages*

(فَصْلٌ) وَالْجِعَالَةُ جَائِزَةٌ، وَهِيَ أَنْ يَشْتَرِطَ فِي رَدِّ ضَالَّتِهِ عِوَضًا مَعْلُومًا. فَإِذَا رَدَّهَا اسْتَحَقَّ ذَلِكَ الْعِوَضَ الْمَشْرُوطَ لَهُ.

Wages are permissible. [For example,] wages are stipulating that whoever returns one's missing property will be given a specific reward. Whoever returns the property deserves the stipulated reward.

7.22 *Sharecropping*

(فَصْلٌ) وَإِذَا دَفَعَ إِلَى رَجُلٍ أَرْضًا لِيَزْرَعَهَا وَشَرَطَ لَهُ جُزْءًا مَعْلُومًا مِنْ رَيْعِهَا لَمْ يَجُزْ. وَإِنْ أَكْرَاهُ إِيَّاهَا بِذَهَبٍ أَوْ فِضَّةٍ أَوْ شَرَطَ لَهُ طَعَامًا مَعْلُومًا فِي ذِمَّتِهِ جَازَ.

Sharecropping is not permissible when [a property owner] presents land to a person to cultivate and stipulates a known portion of its crops [as rent].[12]

It is permissible if the owner rents out the land for gold or silver,[13] or stipulates a known amount of food which becomes a personal debt that the tenant owes.

7.23 *Reviving Abandoned Lands*

(فَصْلٌ) وَإِحْيَاءُ الْمَوَاتِ جَائِزٌ بِشَرْطَيْنِ: أَنْ يَكُونَ الْمُحْيِي مُسْلِمًا، وَأَنْ تَكُونَ الْأَرْضُ حُرَّةً لَمْ يَجْرِ عَلَيْهَا مِلْكٌ لِمُسْلِمٍ. وَصِفَةُ الْإِحْيَاءِ مَا كَانَ فِي الْعَادَةِ عِمَارَةً لِلْمُحْيَا.

It is permissible to revive abandoned lands provided two conditions are met:

a. the one reviving it is a Muslim; and
b. the land is free of buildings [even if run down], and it has not been owned by a Muslim.

Reviving lands takes place by doing whatever is typically needed to build up the abandoned land.

---

12 Imam al-Nawawī followed Ibn Mundhir in considering this to be permissible.
13 It being gold or silver is not a requirement.

7.23.1 Water Rights

وَيَجِبُ بَذْلُ المَاءِ بِثَلَاثَةِ شَرَائِطَ: أَنْ يَفْضُلَ عَنْ حَاجَتِهِ، وَأَنْ يَحْتَاجَ إِلَيْهِ غَيْرُهُ لِنَفْسِهِ أَوْ لِبَهِيمَتِهِ، وَأَنْ يَكُونَ مِمَّا يُسْتَخْلَفُ فِي بِئْرٍ أَوْ عَيْنٍ.

One is obliged to give water [if requested] provided three conditions are met:

a. the water is in excess of one's own needs [including the needs of oneself, one's dependents, animals and crops];
b. for himself or his livestock; and
c. it is located in its well or spring.

7.24 *Endowments*

(فَصْلٌ) وَالْوَقْفُ جَائِزٌ بِثَلَاثَةِ شَرَائِطَ: أَنْ يَكُونَ مِمَّا يُنْتَفَعُ بِهِ مَعَ بَقَاءِ عَيْنِهِ، وَأَنْ يَكُونَ عَلَى أَصْلٍ مَوْجُودٍ وَفَرْعٍ لَا يَنْقَطِعُ، وَأَنْ لَا يَكُونَ فِي مَحْظُورٍ.

وَهُوَ عَلَى مَا شَرَطَ الْوَاقِفُ، مِنْ: تَقْدِيمٍ، وَتَأْخِيرٍ، وَتَسْوِيَةٍ، وَتَفْضِيلٍ.

An endowment is permissible provided three conditions are met:

a. it is something that can be benefitted from without being consumed [and the benefit is lawful];
b. initial recipients exist, and that the future recipients be perpetual;[14]
c. it is not something unlawful.

The endowment must comply with the endower's conditions, including:

14 The preponderant ruling is that it is valid even if the future recipients are not defined. In such a case, it will go to the nearest blood relatives.

1. making some recipients eligible before others; and
2. giving recipients equal or unequal portions.

7.25 *Gifts*

(فَصْلٌ) وَكُلُّ مَا جَازَ بَيْعُهُ جَازَ هِبَتُهُ. وَلَا تَلْزَمُ الْهِبَةُ إِلَّا بِالْقَبْضِ، وَإِذَا قَبَضَهَا الْمَوْهُوبُ لَهُ لَمْ يَكُنْ لِلْوَاهِبِ أَنْ يَرْجِعَ فِيهَا إِلَّا أَنْ يَكُونَ وَالِدًا.

وَإِذَا أَعْمَرَ شَيْئًا أَو أَرْقَبَهُ، كَانَ لِلْمُعْمَرِ أَوْ لِلْمُرْقَبِ وَلِوَرَثَتِهِ مِنْ بَعْدِهِ.

Everything that is permissible to sell is permissible to offer as a gift.

The gift does not become binding until the recipient takes possession of it. Once the recipient takes possession, the one who offered it cannot renege, except in the case of a father taking back a gift from his son.

If someone gives someone something for as long as he lives, or says "If I die first, this is yours," it belongs to the person addressed or his heirs after him.

7.26 *Lost Items*

(فَصْلٌ) وَإِذَا وَجَدَ لُقَطَةً فِي مَوَاتٍ أَوْ طَرِيقٍ فَلَهُ أَخْذُهَا وَتَرْكُهَا، وَأَخْذُهَا أَوْلَى مِنْ تَرْكِهَا إِنْ كَانَ عَلَى ثِقَةٍ مِنَ الْقِيَامِ بِهَا.

وَإِذَا أَخَذَهَا فَعَلَيْهِ أَنْ يَعْرِفَ سِتَّةَ أَشْيَاءَ: وِعَاءَهَا وَعِفَاصَهَا، وَوِكَاءَهَا، وَجِنْسَهَا، وَعَدَدَهَا، وَوَزْنَهَا؛ وَيَحْفَظَهَا فِي حِرْزِ مِثْلِهَا.

ثُمَّ إِذَا أَرَادَ تَمَلُّكَهَا عَرَّفَهَا سَنَةً عَلَى أَبْوَابِ المَسَاجِدِ، وَفِي المَوْضِعِ الَّذِي وَجَدَهَا فِيهِ فَإِنْ لَمْ يَجِدْ صَاحِبَهَا كَانَ لَهُ أَنْ يَتَمَلَّكَهَا بِشَرْطِ الضَّمَانِ.

وَاللُّقَطَةُ عَلَى أَرْبَعَةِ أَضْرُبٍ؛ أَحَدُهَا: مَا يَبْقَى عَلَى الدَّوَامِ، فَهَذَا حُكْمُهُ. وَالثَّانِي: مَا لَا يَبْقَى كَالطَّعَامِ الرَّطْبِ فَهُوَ مُخَيَّرٌ بَيْنَ أَكْلِهِ وَغُرْمِهِ أَوْ بَيْعِهِ وَحِفْظِ ثَمَنِهِ. وَالثَّالِثُ: مَا يَبْقَى بِعِلَاجٍ كَالرُّطَبِ، فَيَفْعَلُ مَا فِيهِ المَصْلَحَةُ مِنْ بَيْعِهِ وَحِفْظِ ثَمَنِهِ أَوْ تَجْفِيفِهِ وَحِفْظِهِ. وَالرَّابِعُ: مَا يَحْتَاجُ إِلَى نَفَقَةٍ كَالْحَيَوَانِ، وَهُوَ ضَرْبَانِ: حَيَوَانٌ لَا يَمْتَنِعُ بِنَفْسِهِ فَهُوَ مُخَيَّرٌ بَيْنَ أَكْلِهِ وَغُرْمِ ثَمَنِهِ، أَوْ تَرْكِهِ وَالتَّطَوُّعِ بِالْإِنْفَاقِ عَلَيْهِ، أَوْ بَيْعِهِ وَحِفْظِ ثَمَنِهِ. وَحَيَوَانٌ يَمْتَنِعُ بِنَفْسِهِ، فَإِنْ وَجَدَهُ فِي الصَّحْرَاءِ تَرَكَهُ، وَإِنْ وَجَدَهُ فِي الْحَضَرِ فَهُوَ مُخَيَّرٌ بَيْنَ الْأَشْيَاءِ الثَّلَاثَةِ فِيهِ.

If one finds a lost item in uninhabited lands or on a path, he may take it or leave it. Taking it is better than leaving it if one is sure that he is trustworthy enough to take care of it.

If one takes the item, he must know six things about the item. [One must know the item's:]

a. exterior;
b. cover;
c. stitching;
d. type;
e. quantity; and
f. weight.

It must be safe-guarded in a place typical for its protection.

If one wants to assume ownership of the item, he must publicize the item for one year. [One does so] on the doors of the mosques [but not inside], and in the vicinity in which the item was found.

If its owner is not found, one is entitled to assume ownership provided one guarantees the item [should the owner later appear].

Found items are of four types:

1. *non-perishable items*: the ruling is as mentioned above.
2. *perishable items, such as foodstuffs and ripe [but not yet dried] dates*: one chooses between eating the item and paying its price, or selling the item and saving the money [for its owner].
3. *items that can be preserved with treatment, such as ripe dates*: one does whatever is in the best interest [of the owner]. This includes selling the item and saving the money, or drying the item and keeping it in storage.
4. *items that require upkeep [and maintenance]* like animals: these items are of two types:
   i. Animals that do not fend for themselves: one chooses between:
      1. eating the animal and paying its price;
      2. not eating it and voluntarily taking care of it; and
      3. selling it and saving the money.
   ii. Animals that fend for themselves: if one finds such an animal in the desert, it is left alone. If one finds it in inhabited areas, one chooses between the three options mentioned above.[15]

7.27 *Foundlings*

(فَصْلٌ) وَإِذَا وُجِدَ لَقِيطٌ بِقَارِعَةِ الطَّرِيقِ فَأَخْذُهُ وَتَرْبِيَتُهُ وَكَفَالَتُهُ وَاجِبَةٌ عَلَى الْكِفَايَةِ، وَلَا يُقَرُّ إِلَّا فِي يَدِ أَمِينٍ. فَإِنْ وُجِدَ مَعَهُ مَالٌ أَنْفَقَ عَلَيْهِ الْحَاكِمُ مِنْهُ، وَإِنْ لَمْ يُوجَدْ مَعَهُ مَالٌ فَنَفَقَتُهُ فِي بَيْتِ الْمَالِ.

15 The preponderant opinion is that the first option does not typically apply in inhabited areas. See al-Jāwī, et al, *Qūt al-Ḥabīb al-Gharīb*, 180.

If one finds an abandoned child in the middle of the street, taking the child in, raising him and looking after him are community obligations.

The child is not left in the charge of anyone except someone who is trustworthy.

If property is found with the child, the judge uses it to pay for the child's expenses. If no property is found with the child, the Muslim Common Fund [*bayt al-māl*] pays for his expenses.

7.28 Deposits for Safekeeping

(فَصْلٌ) الْوَدِيعَةُ أَمَانَةٌ، يُسْتَحَبُّ قَبُولُهَا لِمَنْ قَامَ بِالْأَمَانَةِ فِيهَا، وَلَا يَضْمَنُ إِلَّا بِالتَّعَدِّي. وَقَوْلُ الْمُودَعِ مَقْبُولٌ فِي رَدِّهَا عَلَى الْمُودِعِ، وَعَلَيْهِ أَنْ يَحْفَظَهَا فِي حِرْزِ مِثْلِهَا. وَإِذَا طُولِبَ بِهَا فَلَمْ يُخْرِجْهَا مَعَ الْقُدْرَةِ عَلَيْهَا حَتَّى تَلِفَتْ ضَمِنَ.

A deposit put up for safekeeping is a trust [*amāna*]. It is recommended for someone who will uphold the trust to accept it. [The depositee] is not held liable, except when there is transgression.

The depositee's word is accepted concerning returning the property to the depositor.

The depositee must safeguard the property in the manner typical for the property.

The depositee is liable for damages if the depositor requests the deposit's return and he delays—even though able to do so—until it has been destroyed.

8

INHERITANCE AND BEQUESTS

كِتَابُ الْفَرَائِضِ وَالْوَصَايَا

8.1 *Inheritors*

8.1.1 Male Inheritors

وَالْوَارِثُونَ مِنْ الرِّجَالِ عَشَرَةٌ: الِابْنُ وَابْنُ الِابْنِ وَإِنْ سَفَلَ، وَالْأَبُ وَالْجَدُّ وَإِنْ عَلَا، وَالْأَخُ وَابْنُهُ وَإِنْ تَرَاخَيَا، وَالْعَمُّ وَابْنُهُ وَإِنْ تَبَاعَدَا، وَالزَّوْجُ، وَالْمَوْلَى الْمُعْتِقُ.

There are ten males who inherit:

1. a son;
2. a son's son, however low;
3. the father;
4. the father's father, however high;
5. a brother;
6. a brother's son, however low;
7. a paternal uncle;
8. a paternal uncle's son, however low;
9. the husband; and
10. a male who freed the deceased.

8.1.2 Female Inheritors

وَالْوَارِثَاتُ مِنْ النِّسَاءِ سَبْعٌ: الْبِنْتُ، وَبِنْتُ الِابْنِ، وَالْأُمُّ، وَالْجَدَّةُ وَإِنْ عَلَتْ، وَالْأُخْتُ، وَالزَّوْجَةُ، وَالْمُعْتِقَةُ.

There are seven females who inherit:

1. a daughter;
2. a son's daughter;
3. the mother;
4. a grandmother, however high;
5. a sister;
6. a wife; and
7. a female who freed the deceased.

8.1.3 People Who Always Inherit

وَمَنْ لَا يَسْقُطُ بِحَالٍ خَمْسَةٌ: الزَّوْجَانِ، وَالْأَبَوَانِ، وَوَلَدُ الصُّلْبِ.

Five inheritors are never omitted:

1. the husband;
2. the wife;
3. the father;
4. the mother; and
5. an immediate descendant.

8.1.4 People Who Never Inherit

وَمَنْ لَا يَرِثُ بِحَالٍ سَبْعَةٌ: الْعَبْدُ، وَالْمُدَبَّرُ، وَأُمُّ الْوَلَدِ، وَالْمُكَاتَبُ، وَالْقَاتِلُ، وَالْمُرْتَدُّ، وَأَهْلُ مِلَّتَيْنِ.

Seven never inherit in any circumstance:

1. slaves;
2. a slave who will be freed upon his master's death;
3. a female slave who has borne a child for her master;
4. a slave who is purchasing his freedom;
5. the murderer [who killed the deceased];

6. an apostate; and
7. members of other religions.

8.1.5 Universal Inheritors

وَأَقْرَبُ الْعَصَبَاتِ: الِابْنُ ثُمَّ ابْنُهُ، ثُمَّ الْأَبُ ثُمَّ أَبُوهُ، ثُمَّ الْأَخُ لِلْأَبِ وَالْأُمِّ، ثُمَّ الْأَخُ لِلْأَبِ، ثُمَّ ابْنُ الْأَخِ لِلْأَبِ وَالْأُمِّ، ثُمَّ ابْنُ الْأَخِ لِلْأَبِ، ثُمَّ الْعَمُّ عَلَى هَذَا التَّرْتِيبِ، ثُمَّ ابْنُهُ؛ فَإِنْ عُدِمَتْ الْعَصَبَاتُ فَالْمَوْلَى الْمُعْتِقُ.

Universal inheritors [*'aṣabāt*][1] are [ranked in the following order]:

1. a son;
2. a son's son;
3. the father;
4. the father's father;
5. a full brother;
6. a consanguine brother;[2]
7. a full brother's son;
8. a son of a consanguine brother;
9. a paternal uncle (following the above order); and
10. a paternal uncle's son.

If all of the above are absent, the person who freed the deceased is the universal inheritor [even if female].

8.2 Shares

(فَصْلٌ) وَالْفُرُوضُ الْمُقَدَّرَةُ فِي كِتَابِ اللهِ تَعَالَى سِتَّةٌ: النِّصْفُ، وَالرُّبُعُ، وَالثُّمُنُ، وَالثُّلُثَانِ، وَالثُّلُثُ، وَالسُّدُسُ.

1 Also known as an agnate inheritor.
2 The term "consanguine" indicates a half-sibling from the same father but a different mother.

Six shares are mentioned in the Qur'ān:

1. one-half;
2. one-quarter;
3. one-eighth;
4. two-thirds;
5. one-third; and
6. one-sixth.

8.2.1 One-Half

فَالنِّصْفُ فَرْضُ خَمْسَةٍ: الْبِنْتُ، وَبِنْتُ الِابْنِ إِذَا انْفَرَدَتْ، وَالْأُخْتُ مِنَ الْأَبِ وَالْأُمِّ، وَالْأُخْتُ مِنَ الْأَبِ، وَالزَّوْجُ إِذَا لَمْ يَكُنْ مَعَهُ وَلَدٌ وَلَا وَلَدُ ابْنٍ.

One-half is the obligatory share for five:

1. a daughter;
2. a son's daughter;
3. a full sister;
4. a consanguine sister; and
5. the husband, when no children are present.

8.2.2 One-Quarter

وَالرُّبُعُ فَرْضُ اثْنَيْنِ: الزَّوْجِ مَعَ الْوَلَدِ أَوْ وَلَدِ الِابْنِ، وَهُوَ فَرْضُ الزَّوْجَةِ وَالزَّوْجَاتِ مَعَ عَدَمِ الْوَلَدِ أَوْ وَلَدِ الِابْنِ.

One-quarter is the obligatory share for two:

1. the husband when there is an immediate descendant or a son's descendant; and
2. one or more wives, provided an immediate descendant or a son's descendant is not present.

8.2.3 One-Eighth

وَالثُّمُنُ فَرْضُ الزَّوْجَةِ وَالزَّوْجَاتِ مَعَ الْوَلَدِ أَوْ وَلَدِ الِابْنِ.

One-eighth is the obligatory share for one or more wives, provided an immediate child or a son's descendant is present.

8.2.4 Two-Thirds

وَالثُّلُثَانِ فَرْضُ أَرْبَعَةٍ: البِنْتَيْنِ، وَبِنْتَيْ الِابْنِ، وَالْأُخْتَيْنِ مِنَ الْأَبِ وَالْأُمِّ، وَالْأُخْتَيْنِ مِنَ الْأَبِ.

Two-thirds is the obligatory share for four:

1. two [or more] daughters;
2. two [or more] daughters of a direct son;
3. two [or more] full sisters; and
4. two [or more] consanguine sisters.

8.2.5 One-Third

وَالثُّلُثُ فَرْضُ اثْنَيْنِ: الْأُمِّ إِذَا لَمْ تُحْجَبْ، وَهُوَ لِلِاثْنَيْنِ فَصَاعِدًا مِنَ الْإِخْوَةِ وَالْأَخَوَاتِ مِنْ وَلَدِ الْأُمِّ.

One-third is the obligatory share for two:

1. the mother, provided she is not [partially] inhibited;
2. two or more uterine siblings.[3]

3 The term "uterine" indicates a half-sibling from the same mother but a different father.

8.2.6 One-Sixth

وَالسُّدُسُ فَرْضُ سَبْعَةٍ: الْأُمِّ مَعَ الْوَلَدِ أَوْ وَلَدِ الِابْنِ أَوْ اثْنَيْنِ فَصَاعِدًا مِنْ الْإِخْوَةِ وَالْأَخَوَاتِ، وَهُوَ لِلْجَدَّةِ عَنْدَ عَدَمِ الْأُمِّ، وَلِبِنْتِ الِابْنِ مَعَ بِنْتِ الصُّلْبِ، وَهُوَ لِلْأُخْتِ مِنْ الْأَبِ مَعَ الْأُخْتِ مِنْ الْأَبِ وَالْأُمِّ، وَهُوَ فَرْضُ الْأَبِ مَعَ الْوَلَدِ أَوْ وَلَدِ الِابْنِ، وَفَرْضُ الْجَدِّ عِنْدَ عَدَمِ الْأَبِ، وَهُوَ فَرْضُ الْوَاحِدِ مِنْ وَلَدِ الْأُمِّ.

One-sixth is the obligatory share for seven:

1. the mother, if an immediate descendant, a son's descendant, or two or more siblings are present;
2. the paternal grandmother, provided the mother is not present;
3. the son's daughter, provided an immediate daughter is present;
4. the consanguine sister, provided the full sister is present;
5. the father, provided an immediate descendant or son's descendant is present;
6. the paternal grandfather, if the father is absent; and
7. the mother's child, if the child has no siblings.

8.2.7 Omissions

وَتَسْقُطُ الْجَدَّاتُ بِالْأُمِّ، وَالْأَجْدَادُ بِالْأَبِ. وَيَسْقُطُ وَلَدُ الْأُمِّ مَعَ أَرْبَعَةٍ: الْوَلَدُ، وَوَلَدُ الِابْنِ، وَالْأَبُ، وَالْجَدُّ. وَيَسْقُطُ وَلَدُ الْأَبِ وَالْأُمِّ مَعَ ثَلَاثَةٍ: الِابْنُ، وَابْنُ الِابْنِ، وَالْأَبُ. وَيَسْقُطُ وَلَدُ الْأَبِ بِهَؤُلَاءِ الثَّلَاثَةِ وَبِالْأَخِ مِنْ الْأَبِ وَالْأُمِّ.

The mother's presence causes the grandmother to be omitted.

The father's presence causes the grandfather to be omitted.

The mother's child is omitted in the presence of [one of] four:

1. a son;
2. a son's son;
3. the father; or
4. the [paternal] grandfather.

The full brother is omitted in the presence of [one of] three:

1. a son;
2. a son's son; or
3. the father.

The father's son is omitted by those three, and by the presence of a full brother.

8.2.8 Brothers and Sisters

وَأَرْبَعَةٌ يُعَصِّبُونَ أَخَوَاتِهِمْ: الِابْنُ، وَابْنُ الِابْنِ، وَالْأَخُ مِنَ الْأَبِ وَالْأُمِّ، وَالْأَخُ مِنَ الْأَبِ.

وَأَرْبَعَةٌ يَرِثُونَ دُونَ أَخَوَاتِهِمْ، وَهُمْ: الْأَعْمَامُ، وَبَنُو الْأَعْمَامِ، وَبَنُو الْإِخْوَةِ، وَعَصَبَاتُ الْمَوْلَى الْمُعْتِقِ.

Brothers who [partially] inhibit [the inheritance of] their sisters are four:

1. a son;
2. a son's son;
3. a full brother; and
4. a consanguine brother.

Brothers who inherit while their sisters do not, are four:

1. paternal uncles;
2. sons of paternal uncles;

3. sons of full brothers; and
4. universal inheritors of one who freed a slave.

8.3 Testamentary Bequests and Executors

8.3.1 Testamentary Bequests

(فَصْلٌ) وَتَجُوزُ الْوَصِيَّةُ بِالْمَعْلُومِ وَالْمَجْهُولِ وَالْمَوْجُودِ وَالْمَعْدُومِ وَهِيَ مِنَ الثُّلُثِ، فَإِنْ زَادَ وُقِفَ عَلَى إِجَازَةِ الْوَرَثَةِ. وَلَا تَجُوزُ الْوَصِيَّةُ لِوَارِثٍ إِلَّا أَنْ يُجِيزَهَا بَاقِي الْوَرَثَةِ. وَتَصِحّ الْوَصِيَّةُ مِنْ كُلِّ مَالِكٍ بَالِغٍ عَاقِلٍ لِكُلِّ مُتَمَلِّكٍ وَفِي سَبِيلِ اللهِ تَعَالَى.

It is permissible to bequeath something whether specified or not, currently existing or not.

Testamentary bequests are only permissible when their total is less than or equal to one-third of the estate. [The validity of] bequests exceeding [one-third] is dependent upon consent of the deceased's heirs.

It is not permissible to bequeath something to one of the heirs unless the other heirs permit it.

Bequests are valid from anyone who is mature and of sound mind, to anyone who can own property, or for the sake of Allah Most High.

8.3.2 Executors

وَتَصِحُّ الْوَصِيَّةُ إِلَى مَنِ اجْتَمَعَتْ فِيهِ خَمْسُ خصال: الْإِسْلَامُ، وَالْبُلُوغُ، وَالْعَقْلُ، وَالْحُرِّيَّةُ، وَالْأَمَانَةُ.

It is valid to appoint someone executor if he possesses the following five qualities. [One must be:]

a. a Muslim;[4]
b. mature;
c. of sound mind;
d. free; and
e. trustworthy.

4 The sound opinion is that it is valid for a non-Muslim resident of the Islamic state to appoint another non-Muslim resident of the Islamic state as an executor, provided that the appointed person is considered upright according to their religion.

9

MARRIAGE AND DIVORCE

كِتَابُ النِّكَاحِ وَمَا يَتَعَلَّقُ بِهِ مِنَ الْأَحْكَامِ وَالْقَضَايَا

9.1 *People Who Should Get Married*

وَالنِّكَاحُ مُسْتَحَبٌّ لِمَنْ يَحْتَاجُ إِلَيْهِ، وَيَجُوزُ لِلْحُرِّ أَنْ يَجْمَعَ بَيْنَ أَرْبَعِ حَرَائِرَ، وَلِلْعَبْدِ أَنْ يَجْمَعَ بَيْنَ اثْنَتَيْنِ. وَلَا يَنْكِحُ الْحُرُّ أَمَةً إِلَّا بِشَرْطَيْنِ: عَدَمُ صَدَاقِ الْحُرَّةِ، وَخَوْفُ الْعَنَتِ.

Marriage is recommended for anyone who needs it.

It is permissible for a free man to marry [up to] four free wives, and for a slave to marry two.

A free man does not marry a slave except under two conditions:

a. lack of a free woman's marriage payment; and
b. fear of fornication.[1]

1 There are two other conditions: that he not own a female slave who is a Muslim or from the People of the Book who is lawful for him to have sex with; and that the slave he marries is a Muslim, since it is not permissible for a Muslim to marry a slave who is from the People of the Book.

9.2 *Looking at Members of the Opposite Sex*

وَنَظَرُ الرَّجُلِ إِلَى الْمَرْأَةِ عَلَى سَبْعَةِ أَضْرُبٍ؛ أَحَدُهَا: نَظَرُهُ إِلَى أَجْنَبِيَّةٍ لِغَيْرِ حَاجَةٍ فَغَيْرُ جَائِزٍ. وَالثَّانِي: نَظَرُهُ إِلَى زَوْجَتِهِ وَأَمَتِهِ فَيَجُوزُ أَنْ يَنْظُرَ إِلَى مَا عَدَا الْفَرْجَ منهما. وَالثَّالِثُ: نَظَرُهُ إِلَى ذَوَاتِ مَحَارِمِهِ أَوْ أَمَتِهِ الْمُزَوَّجَةِ فَيَجُوزُ فِيمَا عَدَا مَا بَيْنَ السُّرَّةِ وَالرُّكْبَةِ. وَالرَّابِعُ: النَّظَرُ لِأَجْلِ النِّكَاحِ فَيَجُوزُ إِلَى الْوَجْهِ وَالْكَفَّيْنِ. وَالْخَامِسُ: النَّظَرُ لِلْمُدَاوَاةِ فَيَجُوزُ إِلَى الْمَوَاضِعِ الَّتِي يُحْتَاجُ إِلَيْهَا. وَالسَّادِسُ: النَّظَرُ لِلشَّهَادَةِ أَو لِلْمُعَامَلَةِ فَيَجُوزُ النَّظَرُ إِلَى الْوَجْهِ خَاصَّةً. وَالسَّابِعُ: النَّظَرُ إِلَى الْأَمَةِ عِنْدَ ابْتِيَاعِهَا فَيَجُوزُ إِلَى الْمَوَاضِعِ الَّتِي يَحْتَاجُ إِلَى تَقْلِيبِهَا.

There are seven cases of a man looking at a woman.[2] Looking:

1. *at a unrelated woman without need*: it is impermissible;
2. *at his wife or slave girl*: it is permissible to look at everything other than the genitals;[3]
3. *at close relatives or his married slave girl*: it is permissible to look at everything other than the area between the navel and the knees;
4. *for the purpose of marriage*: it is permissible to look at the face and hands;
5. *for the sake of medical treatment*: it is permissible to look to the extent needed;
6. *for the sake of testimony or trade*: it is permissible to look at the face, specifically; and
7. *at a slave girl when buying her*: it is permissible to look at the areas that need to be inspected.

---

2 In most cases, these rulings similarly apply to women looking at men.

3 The soundest opinion is that it is permissible to look at the genitals, though it is offensive.

9.3 *Integrals*

(فَصْلٌ) وَلَا يَصِحُّ عَقْدُ النِّكَاحِ إِلَّا بِوَلِيٍّ وَشَاهِدَيْ عَدْلٍ.

A marriage contract is invalid without the presence of the bride's guardian and two upright witnesses.

9.3.1 Conditions for the Bride's Guardian and Witnesses

وَيَفْتَقِرُ الْوَلِيُّ وَالشَّاهِدَانِ إِلَى سِتَّةِ شَرَائِطَ: الْإِسْلَامُ، وَالْبُلُوغُ، والْعَقْلُ، وَالْحُرِّيَّةُ، وَالذُّكُورَةُ، وَالْعَدَالَةُ؛ إِلَّا أَنَّهُ لَا يَفْتَقِرُ نِكَاحُ الذِّمِّيَّةِ إِلَى إِسْلَامِ الْوَلِيِّ، وَلَا نِكَاحُ الْأَمَةِ إِلَى عَدَالَةِ السَّيِّدِ.

The bride's guardian and witnesses must meet six conditions. [Each must be:]

a. Muslim;
b. mature;
c. of sound mind;
d. free;
e. male; and
f. upright.

The condition of being Muslim is not required from the bride's guardian when the bride is a non-Muslim resident of the Islamic State. Nor does the owner of a female slave need to be upright [to be her guardian].

9.3.2 The Bride's Guardians

وَأَوْلَى الْوُلَاةِ: الْأَبُ، ثُمَّ الْجَدُّ أَبُو الْأَبِ، ثُمَّ الْأَخُ لِلْأَبِ وَالْأُمِّ، ثُمَّ الْأَخُ لِلْأَبِ، ثُمَّ ابْنُ الْأَخِ لِلْأَبِ وَالْأُمِّ، ثُمَّ ابْنُ الْأَخِ لِلْأَبِ، ثُمَّ الْعَمُّ، ثُمَّ ابْنُهُ عَلَى هَذَا التَّرْتِيبِ. فَإِذَا عُدِمَتِ الْعَصَبَاتُ فَالْمَوْلَى الْمُعْتِقِ، ثُمَّ عَصَبَاتُهُ ثُمَّ الْحَاكِمُ.

Rightful guardianship [for the marriage contract] is determined according to the following order: *obligatory order*

1. the father;
2. the paternal grandfather;
3. a full brother;
4. a consanguine brother;
5. a full brother's son;
6. a consanguine brother's son;
7. a paternal uncle; and
8. a paternal uncle's son.

The rest of the men cannot marry of a woman without her fathers permission.

last on list. *son - cannot be a wali for his mother.*

[When the bride is a former slave:] If a male universal inheritor[4] does not exist, then the guardian is the one who freed her, followed by the emancipator's universal male inheritor.

He is not related to her in terms of lineage. can only if they are from the same tribe.

Then [in the absence of all others], a judge.

According to imam shafi'i ← become

9.3.3 Engagement

وَلَا يَجُوزُ أَنْ يُصَرِّحَ بِخِطْبَةِ مُعْتَدَّةٍ، وَيَجُوزُ أَنْ يُعَرِّضَ لَهَا وَيَنْكِحَهَا بَعْدَ انْقِضَاءِ عِدَّتِهَا.

2 types
- Rajiaa - A man can take her back.
- Non-Rajiya - A man cannot take her back.
Haram to be in a new relationship

It is not permissible to explicitly propose to a woman during her waiting period. It is permissible to allude [to the proposal] and to

Divorced or widowed.

4 See "8.1.5 Universal Inheritors" on page 89.

same for a new muslim woman.

he freer of the slave woman will become her wali → if he passes away, His inheritors will take over. If they aren't available A Judge will take over.

[then] marry her after her [irrevocable] waiting period expires.

9.3.4 Compelling Women to Marry

وَالنِّسَاءُ عَلَى ضَرْبَيْنِ: ثَيِّبَاتٍ، وَأَبْكَارٍ. فَالْبِكْرُ يَجُوزُ لِلْأَبِ وَالْجَدِّ إِجْبَارُهَا عَلَى النِّكَاحِ، وَالثَّيِّبُ لَا يَجُوزُ تَزْوِيجُهَا إِلَّا بَعْدَ بُلُوغِهَا وَإِذْنِهَا.

Women are in two categories:

1. virgins; and
2. non-virgins.

It is permissible for the father or paternal grandfather to compel a virgin to marry.[5]

It is not permissible for them to marry off a non-virgin until she is mature and expresses her consent.

9.3.5 Unmarriageable Women

(فَصْلٌ) وَالْمُحَرَّمَاتُ بِالنَّصِّ أَرْبَعَ عَشْرَةَ، سَبْعٌ بِالنَّسَبِ وَهُنَّ: الْأُمُّ وَإِنْ عَلَتْ، وَالْبِنْتُ وَإِنْ سَفَلَتْ، وَالْأُخْتُ، وَالْخَالَةُ، وَالْعَمَّةُ، وَبِنْتُ الْأَخِ، وَبِنْتُ الْأُخْتِ. وَاثْنَانِ بِالرَّضَاعِ: الْأُمُّ الْمُرْضِعَةُ، وَالْأُخْتُ مِنَ الرَّضَاعِ. وَأَرْبَعٌ بِالْمُصَاهَرَةِ: أُمُّ الزَّوْجَةِ، وَالرَّبِيبَةُ إِذَا دَخَلَ بِالْأُمِّ، وَزَوْجَةُ الْأَبِ، وَزَوْجَةُ الِابْنِ. وَوَاحِدَةٌ مِنْ جِهَةِ الْجَمْعِ وَهِيَ أُخْتُ الزَّوْجَةِ. وَلَا يُجْمَعُ بَيْنَ الْمَرْأَةِ وَعَمَّتِهَا وَلَا بَيْنَ الْمَرْأَةِ وَخَالَتِهَا.

وَيَحْرُمُ مِنَ الرَّضَاعِ مَا يَحْرُمُ مِنَ النَّسَبِ.

---

5 This is valid only when the girl is a virgin, the husband is a suitable match, and the bride's marriage payment is at least equal to that of similar women, and paid using the predominant local currency. However, it is still recommended that her guardian marry her only after obtaining her consent.

There are fourteen women who are unlawful to marry according to textual evidence.

Seven are [unlawful as] a result of kinship. They are:

1. one's mother and her ancestors;
2. one's daughters and their descendants;
3. one's sisters;
4. one's maternal aunts;
5. one's paternal aunts;
6. the daughters of one's brother; and
7. the daughters of one's sister.

Two are [unlawful as] a result of nursing:[6]

1. the mother-through-nursing; and
2. sisters-through-nursing.

Four are [unlawful as] a result of marriage:

1. the wife's mother;
2. the wife's daughter from a previous marriage when one has consummated the marriage to her mother;
3. the wife of one's father; and
4. the wife of one's son.

One is [unlawful] from the perspective of joining: the wife's sister.[7]

One [also] does not join between a woman and her paternal aunt, nor her maternal aunt.

---

6 See "9.14 Nursing" on page 114.

7 What is meant by "joining" is to be married to the wife and someone else concurrently. One cannot be married to two sisters concurrently, though one can marry them consecutively.

Whatever is unlawful with blood relatives is also unlawful with relatives through nursing.

9.3.6 Spousal Defects Permitting Annulment

وَتُرَدُّ الْمَرْأَةُ بِخَمْسَةِ عُيُوبٍ: بِالْجُنُونِ، وَالْجُذَامِ، وَالْبَرَصِ، وَالرَّتْقِ، وَالْقَرَنِ. وَيُرَدُّ الرَّجُلُ بِخَمْسَةِ عُيُوبٍ: بِالْجُنُونِ، وَالْجُذَامِ، وَالْبَرَصِ، وَالْجَبِّ، وَالْعُنَّةِ.

A woman can be rejected because of five defects:

1. insanity;
2. leprosy;
3. vitiligo;[8] and
4. vaginal constriction because of flesh, or
5. because of bone.

A man can be rejected because of five defects:

1. insanity;
2. leprosy;
3. vitiligo;
4. a severed penis; or
5. impotence.

9.3.7 The Wife's Marriage Payment - sataaq.

(فَصْلٌ) ويُستَحَبُّ تَسمِيَةُ المَهرِ فِي النِّكَاحِ، فَإِنْ لَمْ يُسَمَّ صَحَّ الْعَقْدُ وَوَجَبَ المَهْرُ بِثَلَاثَةِ أَشْيَاءَ: أَنْ يَفْرِضَهُ الزَّوْجُ عَلَى نَفْسِهِ، أَوْ يَفْرِضَهُ الحَاكِمُ، أَوْ يَدْخُلَ بِهَا، فَيَجِبُ مَهْرُ المِثْلِ.

Doesn't have to be mentioned - only sunnah.

---

8 The Arabic is *baraṣ*. Ibn Qāsim describes this as a sickness where the skin turns white and blood ceases circulating in the skin, causing the tissues to die. This is not the same as *bahaq*, where the skin changes color without loss of tissue. Lack of pigment in and of itself is not enough.

If maher isn't agreed upon.
- Husband say I will pay you x amount
- The judge will make a judgment if cann[ot] be agreed on by looking at her status.

وَلَيْسَ لِأَقَلِّ الصَّدَاقِ وَلَا لِأَكْثَرِهِ حَدٌّ. وَيَجُوزُ أَنْ يَتَزَوَّجَهَا عَلَى مَنْفَعَةٍ مَعْلُومَةٍ.
وَيَسْقُطُ بِالطَّلَاقِ قَبْلَ الدُّخُولِ نِصْفُ المَهْرِ.

It is recommended to state the [amount of the] marriage payment in the contract. If it is not stated, the contract is valid and the marriage payment is determined by [one of] three things [happening]:

a. the husband obligating himself to a specific amount [and she accepts];
b. the judge obligating a specific amount; or
c. the consummation of the marriage, in which case what similar women get becomes obligatory.

There is no minimum amount for the marriage payment, nor is there a maximum limit.

It is permissible to marry a woman using a known utility [as the marriage payment].

The marriage payment is reduced by half if the husband divorces her before consummation.

9.4 *The Wedding Feast*

(فَصْلٌ) وَالْوَلِيمَةُ عَلَى العُرْسِ مُسْتَحَبَّةٌ، وَالْإِجَابَةُ إِلَيْهَا وَاجِبَةٌ إِلَّا مِنْ عُذْرٍ.

A feast for the wedding is recommended. It is obligatory to answer the invitation, unless one has an excuse.

9.5 *Giving Wives Equal Time*

(فَصْلٌ) وَالتَّسْوِيَةُ فِي الْقَسْمِ بَيْنَ الزَّوْجَاتِ وَاجِبَةٌ، وَلَا يَدْخُلُ عَلَى غَيْرِ الْمَقْسُومِ لَهَا لِغَيْرِ حَاجَةٍ. وَإِذَا أَرَادَ السَّفَرَ أَقْرَعَ بَيْنَهُنَّ وَخَرَجَ بِالَّتِي تَخْرُجُ عَلَيْهَا الْقُرْعَةُ. وَإِذَا تَزَوَّجَ جَدِيدَةً خَصَّهَا بِسَبْعِ لَيَالٍ إِنْ كَانَتْ بِكْرًا، وَبِثَلَاثٍ إِنْ كَانَتْ ثَيِّبًا.

It is obligatory to give each wife an equal portion of time. The husband does not visit a wife [at night] if it is not her turn, except when necessary.

If he wants to travel, they draw lots and he goes with the one whose lot is drawn.

If he marries a new wife, he spends seven nights with her if she is a virgin, and three if she is a non-virgin.

9.5.1 A Disobedient Wife

وَإِذَا خَافَ نُشُوزَ الْمَرْأَةِ وَعَظَهَا، فَإِنْ أَبَتْ إِلَّا النُّشُوزَ هَجَرَهَا، فَإِنْ أَقَامَتْ عَلَيْهِ ضَرَبَهَا، وَيَسْقُطُ بِالنُّشُوزِ قَسْمُهَا وَنَفَقَتُهَا.

If the husband suspects that the wife is being disobedient,[9] he warns her. If she refuses to desist, he ceases sleeping with her. If she persists in being disobedient, he ceases sleeping with her and [lightly] strikes her.[10]

Her allocated portion of time and support stops being obligatory as a result of her disobedience.

---

9 Disobedience means that she ceases performing the *finite* duties that Allah has made obligatory on her with respect to her husband.

10 She is struck for the sake of discipline, not injury. If the husband knows that striking her is pointless, it is unlawful for him to do so. If striking results in injury, he must pay her compensation.

9.6 *Release for Compensation*

(فَصْلٌ) وَالْخُلْعُ جَائِزٌ عَلَى عِوَضٍ مَعْلُومٍ. وَتَمْلِكُ الْمَرْأَةُ بِهِ نَفْسَهَا وَلَا رَجْعَةَ لَهُ عَلَيْهَا إِلَّا بِنِكَاحٍ جَدِيدٍ. وَيَجُوزُ الْخُلْعُ فِي الطُّهْرِ وَالْحَيْضِ، وَلَا يَلْحَقُ الْمُخْتَلِعَةَ الطَّلَاقُ.

It is permissible for a husband to release his wife in exchange for a known item or service.[11] Through it the woman takes sole control of herself, and the husband is not entitled to take her back without a new contract.

Release for compensation is permissible during times of purity and menstruation.

A woman who has been released for compensation cannot be divorced.

9.7 *Divorce*

(فَصْلٌ) وَالطَّلَاقُ ضَرْبَانِ: صَرِيحٌ، وَكِنَايَةٌ. فَالصَّرِيحُ ثَلَاثَةُ أَلْفَاظٍ: الطَّلَاقُ، وَالْفِرَاقُ، وَالسَّرَاحُ؛ ولا يفتقِرُ صَرِيْحُ الطَّلَاقِ إلى النِّيَّة. وَالْكِنَايَةُ كُلُّ لَفْظٍ احْتَمَلَ الطَّلَاقَ وَغَيْرَهُ وَتَفْتَقِرُ إِلَى النِّيَّةِ.

Divorce is of two types [with respect to the phrases used]:

1. explicit; and
2. allusive.

Three phrases are explicit:

1. "divorce;"
2. "separation;" and

---

11 This type of separation counts as a single, irrevocable divorce.

3. "parting."[12]

Explicit phrases do not require intention [in order for a divorce to take place].

Phrases which convey a meaning in addition to divorce are allusive. Allusive phrases require intention [in order for a divorce to occur].

9.7.1 Sunnah and Bid'ah Divorce

وَالنِّسَاءُ فِيهِ ضَرْبَانِ: ضَربٌ فِي طلاقِهِنَّ سُنَّةٌ وبِدْعَةٌ، وهُنَّ ذوَاتُ الْحَيْضِ. فالسُّنَّة أَنْ يُوقِعَ الطَّلَاقَ في طُهْرٍ غَيْرِ مُجَامِعٍ فِيهِ. وَالبِدْعَةُ أَنْ يُوقِعَ الطَّلَاقَ فِي الْحَيْضِ، أَوْ فِي طُهْرٍ جَامَعَهَا فِيهِ. وَضَرْبٌ لَيْسَ فِي طَلَاقِهِنَّ سُنَّةٌ وَلَا بِدْعَةٌ، وَهُنَّ أَرْبَعٌ: الصَّغِيرَةُ، وَالْآيِسَةُ، وَالْحَامِلُ، وَالْمُخْتَلِعَةُ الَّتِي لَمْ يَدْخُلْ بِهَا.

Women are in two categories with respect to divorce.

1. Those for whom divorce can be *sunnah* and *bid'ah*: they are women who menstruate. The *sunnah* is the divorce taking place during a period of purity in which intercourse has not occurred. The *bid'ah* is the divorce taking place during menstruation, or a period of purity in which intercourse has occurred.
2. Those for whom there is no *sunnah* or *bid'ah* for their divorce: they are four. A woman who:
    1. is immature;
    2. is menopausal;
    3. is pregnant; or
3. has gained release through compensation prior to consummation.

12 In English, only the first phrase ("divorce") is necessarily explicit. The others are allusive.

9.7.2 Number of Divorces — طلاق – *Divorce*

(فَصْلٌ) وَيَمْلِكُ الْحُرُّ ثَلَاثَ تَطْلِيقَاتٍ وَالْعَبْدُ تَطْلِيقَتَيْنِ. وَيَصِحُّ الِاسْتِثْنَاءُ فِي الطَّلَاقِ إِذَا وَصَلَهُ بِهِ وَيَصِحُّ تَعْلِيقُهُ بِالصِّفَةِ وَالشَّرْطِ. وَلَا يَقَعُ الطَّلَاقُ قَبْلَ النِّكَاحِ.

وَأَرْبَعٌ لَا يَقَعُ طَلَاقُهُمْ: الصَّبِيُّ، وَالْمَجْنُونُ، وَالنَّائِمُ، وَالْمُكْرَهُ.

I divorce you x3 except
x3 - means there's nothing left i.e. divorced for good.

A free man possesses (three) divorces. A slave possesses (two).

It is valid to make an exception when pronouncing a divorce provided it is connected to the pronouncement.[13]

A man can say I have divorced you x3 except x1
or else not valid. must be said all together.

It is also valid to make divorce contingent upon [the occurrence
of] an attribute or condition.

if I see you again in this house I have... e.g. only
e.g. Begining of Ramadan I have divorced you. divorced divorced x2

Pronouncing divorce prior to the marriage does not take effect.

extreme abnormal anger & divorce is mentioned
this is not accepted.

Divorce [initiated] from **Four** [kinds of husbands] does not take
effect. [When he is:]

1. immature; — السبي - *Hasn't reached pubity*
2. insane;
3. asleep; or
4. coerced to do so. → *forced to divorced e.g. by brothers/father.*

Divorce before marriage is invalid.

9.8 *Taking Back One's Wife*

(فَصْلٌ) وَإِذَا طَلَّقَ الْحُرُّ امْرَأَتَهُ وَاحِدَةً أَوْ ثِنْتَيْنِ فَلَهُ مُرَاجَعَتُهَا مَا لَمْ تَنْقَضِ عِدَّتُهَا، فَإِذَا انْقَضَتْ عِدَّتُهَا كَانَ لَهُ نِكَاحُهَا بِعَقْدٍ جَدِيدٍ وَتَكُونُ مَعَهُ عَلَى مَا بَقِيَ مِنَ الطَّلَاقِ.

---

[13] An additional condition is that the excepted amount not encompass the
original amount. So while "Three except for two" results in a single divorce,
"Three minus three" results in the original amount since the exception is
invalid.

A husband doesn't need permission to take her back after her divorce

Returning/ to take back — الرجع
Surah Baqrah 228

Returning a women who is in her waiting period from a non-finalised or non 3 fold divorce to the state of marriage

فَإِنْ طَلَّقَهَا ثَلَاثًا لَمْ تَحِلَّ لَهُ إِلَّا بَعْدَ وُجُودِ خَمْسَةِ شَرَائِطَ: انْقِضَاءُ عِدَّتِهَا مِنْهُ، وَتَزْوِيجُهَا بِغَيْرِهِ، وَدُخُولُهُ بِهَا وَإِصَابَتُهَا، وَبَيْنُونَتُهَا مِنْهُ، وَانْقِضَاءُ عِدَّتِهَا مِنْهُ.

If the husband has divorced his wife once or twice, he may take her back as long as her waiting period has not expired.[14] If the waiting period expires, he can marry her with a new contract; she will return with whatever [number of] divorces remain.

If he divorces her three times, she remains unlawful for him until five conditions are met:

a. her waiting period from him expires;
b. another man marries her;
c. the [new] marriage is consummated;
d. she is divorced from the new husband; and
e. her waiting period [from the new husband] expires.

9.9 *Forswearing One's Wife*

(فَصْلٌ) وَإِذَا حَلَفَ أَنْ لَا يَطَأَ زَوْجَتَهُ مُطْلَقًا أَوْ مُدَّةً تَزِيدُ عَلَى أَرْبَعَةِ أَشْهُرٍ فَهُوَ مُولٍ. وَيُؤَجَّلُ لَهُ إِنْ سَأَلَتْ ذَلِكَ أَرْبَعَةَ أَشْهُرٍ ثُمَّ يُخَيَّرُ بَيْنَ الْفَيْئَةِ وَالتَّكْفِيرِ، أَوْ الطَّلَاقِ؛ فَإِنْ امْتَنَعَ طَلَّقَ عَلَيْهِ الْحَاكِمُ.

If the husband forswears having intercourse with his wife forever or for a period exceeding four months, he has [indeed] forsworn her. If she requests [separation], he is left alone for four months. He then chooses between breaking his oath and making an expiation, or divorce. If he refuses, the judge issues a divorce for him.

---

14 This must be stated verbally. Intimate contact is not itself enough.

9.10 *Likening One's Wife to One's Mother*

(فَصْلٌ) وَالظِّهَارُ أَنْ يَقُولَ الرَّجُلُ لِزَوْجَتِهِ: «أَنْتِ عَلَيَّ كَظَهْرِ أُمِّي»، فَإِذَا قَالَ ذَلِكَ وَلَمْ يُتْبِعْهُ بِالطَّلَاقِ صَارَ عَائِدًا، وَلَزِمَتْهُ الْكَفَّارَةُ.

Likening one's wife to one's mother [*ẓihār*] is when a man says to his wife, "To me, you are akin to my mother." If he says this and does not follow it with a divorce, he has reneged [gone against his comparison] and must make an expiation.[15]

9.10.1 The Expiation

وَالْكَفَّارَةُ: عِتْقُ رَقَبَةٍ مُؤْمِنَةٍ سَلِيمَةٍ مِنَ الْعُيُوبِ الْمُضِرَّةِ بِالْعَمَلِ وَالْكَسْبِ، فَإِنْ لَمْ يَجِدْ فَصِيَامُ شَهْرَيْنِ مُتَتَابِعَيْنِ، فَإِنْ لَمْ يَسْتَطِعْ فَإِطْعَامُ سِتِّينَ مِسْكِينًا، كُلُّ مِسْكِينٍ مُدٌّ. وَلَا يَحِلُّ وَطْؤُهَا حَتَّى يُكَفِّرَ.

The expiation is emancipating a Muslim slave free from defects which would prevent the slave from working and earning [a living].

If one is not found, the husband fasts two months consecutively.

If he is unable [to fast the two months], he gives food to 60 of the poor, one *mudd* to each.

It is not permissible to have intercourse with the wife until the expiation is made.

---

15 The same applies when the wife is likened to any other of his female kin. These rulings do not apply if the comparison was intended as praise.

9.11 *Charging One's Wife With Adultery*

(فَصْلٌ) وَإِذَا رَمَى الرَّجُلُ زَوْجَتَهُ بِالزِّنَا فَعَلَيْهِ حَدُّ الْقَذْفِ إِلَّا أَنْ يُقِيمَ الْبَيِّنَةَ أَوْ يُلَاعِنُ، فَيَقُولُ عِنْدَ الْحَاكِمِ فِي الْجَامِعِ عَلَى الْمِنْبَرِ فِي جَمَاعَةٍ مِنَ النَّاسِ: «أَشْهَدُ بِاللهِ إِنَّنِي لَمِنَ الصَّادِقِينَ فِيمَا رَمَيْتُ بِهِ زَوْجَتِي مِنَ الزِّنَا وَإِنَّ هَذَا الْوَلَدَ مِنَ الزِّنَا وَلَيْسَ مِنِّي» أَرْبَعَ مَرَّاتٍ، وَيَقُولُ فِي الْخَامِسَةِ بَعْدَ أَنْ يَعِظَهُ الْحَاكِمُ: «وَعَلَيَّ لَعْنَةُ اللهِ إِنْ كُنْتُ مِنَ الْكَاذِبِينَ».

وَيَتَعَلَّقُ بِلِعَانِهِ خَمْسَةُ أَحْكَامٍ: سُقُوطُ الْحَدِّ عَنْهُ، وَوُجُوبُ الْحَدِّ عَلَيْهَا، وَزَوَالُ الْفِرَاشِ، وَنَفْيُ الْوَلَدِ، وَالتَّحْرِيمُ عَلَى الْأَبَدِ.

وَيَسْقُطُ الْحَدُّ عَنْهَا بِأَنْ تُلَاعِنَ فَتَقُولُ: «أَشْهَدُ بِاللهِ أَنَّ فُلَانًا هَذَا لَمِنَ الْكَاذِبِينَ فِيمَا رَمَانِي بِهِ مِنَ الزِّنَا» أَرْبَعَ مَرَّاتٍ، وَتَقُولُ فِي الْخَامِسَةِ بَعْدَ أَنْ يَعِظَهَا الْحَاكِمُ: «وَعَلَيَّ غَضَبُ اللهِ إِنْ كَانَ مِنَ الصَّادِقِينَ».

If a husband charges his wife with adultery, he is subject to punishment for charging another with adultery unless he brings proof or makes a public imprecation [*mulāʿina*] against her.

[If he chooses to make public imprecation], he says while in the presence of the judge and a group, while standing on the *minbar*:[16]

> I bear witness to Allah that I am truthful in charging my wife so-and-so with fornication, and that this child is a product of adultery and not mine.

[He says this] four times. The fifth time, after the judge warns him [of the consequences of lying], he says:

---

16 Standing on the *minbar* is recommended, not required.

> ...and may the curse of Allah be upon me if I am a liar.

Five rulings are associated with his public imprecation:

1. he is no longer subject to punishment [for charging his wife with adultery];
2. the wife becomes subject to punishment [for adultery];
3. the marriage is terminated;
4. the child is negated; and
5. eternally unlawful [to one another].

She ceases being subject to punishment [for adultery] if she performs a counter-imprecation by saying:

> I bear witness that so-and-so is a liar in his charging me with adultery.

[She says this] four times. The fifth time, after the judge warns her [of the consequences of lying], she says:

> ...and may the wrath of Allah be upon me if I am a liar.

9.12 *The Waiting Period*

(فَصْلٌ) وَالْمُعْتَدَّةُ عَلَى ضَرْبَيْنِ: مُتَوَفًّى عَنْهَا، وَغَيْرُ مُتَوَفًّى عَنْهَا.

There are two categories of women with respect to the waiting period:

1. widows; and
2. non-widows.

9.12.1 Widows

فَالْمُتَوَفَّى عَنْهَا: إِنْ كَانَتْ حَامِلًا فَعِدَّتُهَا بِوَضْعِ الْحَمْلِ، وَإِنْ كَانَتْ حَائِلًا فَعِدَّتُهَا أَرْبَعَةُ أَشْهُرٍ وَعَشْرٌ.

If the widow is:

1. *pregnant*: her waiting period [expires] upon delivery [of the child];[17]
2. *not pregnant*: her waiting period is four [lunar] months and ten [days].

9.12.2 Non-Widows

وَغَيْرُ الْمُتَوَفَّى عَنْهَا: إِنْ كَانَتْ حَامِلًا فَعِدَّتُهَا بِوَضْعِ الْحَمْلِ، وَإِنْ كَانَتْ حَائِلًا وَهِيَ مِنْ ذَوَاتِ الْحَيْضِ فَعِدَّتُهَا ثَلَاثَةُ قُرُوءٍ وَهِيَ الْأَطْهَارُ، وَإِنْ كَانَتْ صَغِيرَةً أَوْ آيِسَةً فَعِدَّتُهَا ثَلَاثَةُ أَشْهُرٍ. وَالْمُطَلَّقَةُ قَبْلَ الدُّخُولِ بِهَا لَا عِدَّةَ عَلَيْهَا.

If the non-widow is:

1. *pregnant*: her waiting period [expires] upon delivery;[18]
2. *not pregnant and she has menstrual periods*: her waiting period is three periods of purity [between menstruations];
3. *immature or menopausal*: her waiting period is three [lunar] months.

If the divorce occurred before the marriage was consummated, there is no waiting period.

17 This is provided that it is possible that the husband is the child's father.
18 This is provided that the husband is the child's father.

9.12.3 Slaves

وَعِدَّةُ الْأَمَةِ بِالْحَمْلِ كَعِدَّةِ الْحُرَّةِ، وَبِالْأَقْرَاءِ أَنْ تَعْتَدَّ بِقُرْأَيْنِ، وَبِالشُّهُورِ عَنِ الْوَفَاةِ أَنْ تَعْتَدَّ بِشَهْرَيْنِ وَخَمْسَةِ أَيَّامٍ، وَعَنِ الطَّلَاقِ بِشَهْرٍ وَنِصْفٍ، فَإِنِ اعْتَدَّتْ بِشَهْرَيْنِ كَانَ أَوْلَى.

A slave's waiting period based on:

1. *pregnancy*: is the same as that of a free woman;[19]
2. *periods of purity*: is two periods of purity [not three];
3. *months, because of death*: is two [lunar] months and five nights;
4. *months, because of divorce*: is one and a half [lunar] months, though it is best if she waits for two months.

(فَصْلٌ) وَيَجِبُ لِلْمُعْتَدَّةِ الرَّجْعِيَّةِ السُّكْنَى وَالنَّفَقَةُ، وَيَجِبُ لِلْبَائِنِ السُّكْنَى دُونَ النَّفَقَةِ إِلَّا أَنْ تَكُونَ حَامِلًا.

9.12.4 Support and Maintenance

[During the waiting period,] housing and expenses are obligatory [for the husband to provide] to a woman who can be taken back. Housing (without expenses) is obligatory [for the husband to provide] to a woman who has been irrevocably divorced, unless she is pregnant.

9.12.5 Mourning

وَيَجِبُ عَلَى الْمُتَوَفَّى عَنْهَا زَوْجُهَا الْإِحْدَادُ وَهُوَ الِامْتِنَاعُ مِنَ الزِّينَةِ وَالطِّيبِ، وَعَلَى الْمُتَوَفَّى عَنْهَا وَالْمَبْتُوتَةِ مُلَازَمَةُ الْبَيْتِ إِلَّا لِحَاجَةٍ.

---

19 This is provided that the owner is the child's father.

A widow must observe mourning [*iḥdād*], which is refraining from adornment and using perfume.

A widow and an irrevocably divorced woman must remain in the house, except in cases of necessity.

9.13 *Buying a Slave Girl*

(فَصْلٌ) وَمَنِ اسْتَحْدَثَ مِلْكَ أَمَةٍ حَرُمَ عَلَيْهِ الِاسْتِمْتَاعُ بِهَا حَتَّى يَسْتَبْرِئَهَا: إِنْ كَانَتْ مِنْ ذَوَاتِ الْحَيْضِ بِحَيْضَةٍ، وَإِنْ كَانَتْ مِنْ ذَوَاتِ الشُّهُورِ بِشَهْرٍ، وَإِنْ كَانَتْ مِنْ ذَوَاتِ الْحَمْلِ بِالْوَضْعِ. وَإِذَا مَاتَ سَيِّدُ أُمِّ الْوَلَدِ اسْتَبْرَأَتْ نَفْسَهَا كَالْأَمَةِ.

It is unlawful for someone assuming ownership of a slave girl to have intimate contact with her until making sure that she is not pregnant.

If her waiting period is determined by:

1. *menstruation*: it is a single menstruation;
2. *months*: it is just one [lunar] month;
3. *delivery*: it is by delivery.

If the master of a slave who has borne his child[20] dies, she does the foregoing [to ensure that she is not pregnant] on her own. It is based on [the times for] a slave.

9.14 *Nursing*

(فَصْلٌ) وَإِذَا أَرْضَعَتْ الْمَرْأَةُ بِلَبَنِهَا وَلَدًا صَارَ الرَّضِيعُ وَلَدَهَا بِشَرْطَيْنِ؛ أَحَدُهُمَا: أَنْ يَكُونَ لَهُ دُونَ الْحَوْلَيْنِ. وَالثَّانِي أَنْ تُرْضِعَهُ خَمْسَ رَضَعَاتٍ مُتَفَرِّقَاتٍ وَيَصِيرُ زَوْجُهَا أَبًا لَهُ.

---

20 See "17.5 *Umm al-Walad*" on page 160.

وَيَحْرُمُ عَلَى الْمُرْضَعِ التَّزْوِيجُ إِلَيْهَا وَإِلَى كُلِّ مَنْ نَاسَبَهَا، وَيَحْرُمُ عَلَيْهَا التَّزْوِيجُ إِلَيْهِ وَوَلَدِهِ دُونَ مَنْ كَانَ فِي دَرَجَتِهِ أَوْ أَعْلَى طَبَقَةً مِنْهُ.

If a woman nurses a child with her milk, the child becomes [akin to] her [own] child under two conditions:

a. the child is less than two [lunar] years in age; and
b. she nurses him five separate times.

Her husband becomes [akin to] a father to him.

It is unlawful for a child-through-nursing to marry his nurse-mother and her kin.

It is unlawful for the mother-through-nursing to be married to her son-through-nursing and his children, but not to his siblings or ancestors.

9.15 *Support*

(فَصْلٌ) وَنَفَقَةُ العَمُودَيْنِ مِنَ الْأَهْلِ وَاجِبَةٌ لِلْوَالِدِينَ وَالْمَوْلُودِينَ. فَأَمَّا الْوَالِدُونَ فَتَجِبُ نَفَقَتُهُمْ بِشَرْطَيْنِ: الْفَقْرُ وَالزَّمَانَةُ، أَوْ الْفَقْرُ وَالْجُنُونُ؛ وَأَمَّا الْمَوْلُودُونَ فَتَجِبُ نَفَقَتُهُمْ بِثَلَاثَةِ شَرَائِطَ: الْفَقْرُ وَالصِّغَرُ، أَوْ الْفَقْرُ وَالزَّمَانَةُ، أَوْ الْفَقْرُ وَالْجُنُونُ.

وَنَفَقَةُ الرَّقِيقِ وَالْبَهَائِمِ وَاجِبَةٌ، وَلَا يُكَلَّفُونَ مِنْ الْعَمَلِ مَا لَا يُطِيقُونَ.

It is obligatory for parents and children to support their ancestors and descendants.

Supporting parents is obligatory under two conditions:

1. poverty[21] combined with old age; or
2. poverty combined with insanity.

Supporting children is obligatory under three conditions:

1. poverty combined with immaturity;
2. poverty combined with old age; or
3. poverty combined with insanity.

Support for one's slaves and animals is obligatory. They are not held responsible for work they are incapable of performing.

9.15.1 Spousal Support

وَنَفَقَةُ الزَّوْجَةِ الْمُمَكِّنَةِ مِنْ نَفْسِهَا وَاجِبَةٌ، وَهِيَ مُقَدَّرَةٌ: فَإِنْ كَانَ الزَّوْجُ مُوسِرًا فَمُدَّانِ مِنْ غَالِبِ قُوتِهَا، وَيَجِبُ لَهَا مِنَ الْأُدْمِ وَالْكِسْوَةِ مَا جَرَتْ بِهِ الْعَادَةُ؛ وَإِنْ كَانَ مُعْسِرًا فَمُدٌّ مِنْ غَالِبِ قُوتِ الْبَلَدِ وَمَا يَتَأَدَّمُ بِهِ الْمُعْسِرُونَ وَيَكْسُونَهُ؛ وَإِنْ كَانَ مُتَوَسِّطًا فَمُدٌّ وَنِصْفٌ وَمِنَ الْأُدْمِ وَالْكِسْوَةِ الْوَسَطُ. وَإِنْ كَانَتْ مِمَّنْ يُخْدَمُ مِثْلُهَا فَعَلَيْهِ إِخْدَامُهَا. وَإِنْ أَعْسَرَ بِنَفَقَتِهَا فَلَهَا فَسْخُ النِّكَاحِ، وَكَذَلِكَ إِنْ أَعْسَرَ بِالصَّدَاقِ قَبْلَ الدُّخُولِ.

It is obligatory to support one's wife if she makes herself available to him.

Its [minimum] amount [is as follows]:

If *the husband is well-off*: two *mudd* [1.02 liters] of the predominantly stored foodstuffs of the region, whatever is typically eaten with bread, and whatever is typically worn.

21 Here, poverty means lack of funds or not finding work.

If *the husband is poor*: one *mudd* [0.51 liters] of the predominantly stored foodstuffs, whatever is typically eaten with bread and typically worn by the poor.

If *the husband is between the two*: 1 1/2 *mudd* [0.765 liters] of the predominantly stored foodstuffs, food eaten with bread and clothes that are [typically worn by people of this class].

If someone such as her typically has servants, then she is provided with a servant.

If he is unable to provide [for future] upkeep, she may [ask a judge to] annul the marriage.[22] She may do the same if he is unable to provide the marriage payment prior to consummation.

9.16 Custody

(فَصْلٌ) وَإِذَا فَارَقَ الرَّجُلُ زَوْجَتَهُ وَلَهُ مِنْهَا وَلَدٌ فَهِيَ أَحَقُّ بِحَضَانَتِهِ إِلَى سَبْعِ سِنِيْنَ، ثُمَّ يُخَيَّرُ بَيْنَ أَبَوَيْهِ، فَأَيُّهُمَا اخْتَارَهُ سُلِّمَ إِلَيْهِ.

وَشَرَائِطُ الْحَضَانَةِ سَبْعَةٌ: الْعَقْلُ، والْحُرِّيَّةُ، وَالدِّينُ، وَالْعِفَّةُ، وَالْأَمَانَةُ، وَالْإِقَامَةُ، وَالْخُلُوُّ مِنْ زَوْجٍ؛ فَإِنْ اخْتَلَّ مِنْهَا شَرْطٌ سَقَطَتْ.

If a man separates from his wife and they have an infant, she has the most right to the infant's custody until he is seven [lunar] years old. The child then chooses between his parents and is presented to whomever he chooses.

The conditions for custody are seven. [The custodian must be:]

a. of sound mind;
b. free;

22 She can also choose to be patient and seek compensation for whatever expenses she pays.

c. a Muslim;
d. chaste;
e. trustworthy;
f. a resident; and
g. single [if the mother].

Custody ceases whenever one of these conditions is absent.

10

INJURIOUS CRIMES

كِتَابُ الْجِنَايَاتِ

10.1 *Types of Wrongful Killing*

الْقَتْلُ عَلَى ثَلَاثَةِ أَضْرُبٍ: عَمْدٍ مَحْضٍ، وَخَطَأٍ مَحْضٍ، وَعَمْدٍ خَطَأٍ. فَالْعَمْدُ الْمَحْضُ هُوَ: أَنْ يَعْمِدَ إِلَى ضَرْبِهِ بِمَا يَقْتُلُ غَالِبًا وَيَقصِدَ قَتْلَهُ بِذَلِكَ فَيَجِبُ الْقَوَدُ عَلَيْهِ، فَإِنْ عَفَا عَنْهُ وَجَبَ دِيَةٌ مُغَلَّظَةٌ حَالَّةٌ فِي مَالِ الْقَاتِلِ. وَالْخَطَأُ الْمَحْضُ: أَنْ يرمِيَ إِلَى شَيْءٍ فَيُصِيبَ رَجُلًا فَيَقْتُلَهُ فَلَا قَوَدَ عَلَيْهِ، بَلْ تَجِبُ دِيَةٌ مُخَفَّفَةٌ عَلَى الْعَاقِلَةِ مُؤَجَّلَةٌ فِي ثَلَاثِ سِنِينَ. وَعَمْدُ الْخَطَأِ: أَنْ يَقْصِدَ ضَرْبَهُ بِمَا لَا يَقْتُلُ غَالِبًا فَيَمُوتُ فلا قَوَدَ عَلَيْهِ، بَلْ تَجِبُ دِيَةٌ مُغَلَّظَةٌ عَلَى العاقِلَة، مُؤَجَّلَةٌ فِي ثَلَاثِ سِنِيْنَ.

There are three types of [wrongful] killing:

1. purely intentional;
2. a mistake made in a deliberate injury; and
3. an honest mistake.

Purely intentional is when one deliberately strikes with something that usually kills, and does so with the intention to kill. A reciprocal killing is obligatory. If he is forgiven, then an augmented indemnity is obligatory, due immediately from the killer's property.

A *mistake made in a deliberate injury* is when, [for example,] one shoots at something, and hits a man, fatally. Here, there is no reciprocal killing; instead, his male relatives pay a reduced indemnity over a span of three years.

An *honest mistake* is when one deliberately strikes someone with something that is not usually lethal, yet the person dies. [For this,] there is no reciprocal killing; instead, an augmented indemnity is paid over three years.

10.1.1 Conditions for Reciprocal Punishment

وَشَرَائِطُ وُجُوبِ الْقِصَاصِ أَرْبَعَةٌ: أَنْ يَكُونَ الْقَاتِلُ بَالِغًا عَاقِلًا، وَأَنْ لَا يَكُونَ وَالِدًا لِلْمَقْتُولِ، وَأَنْ لَا يَكُونَ الْمَقْتُولُ أَنْقَصَ مِنَ الْقَاتِلِ بِكُفْرٍ أَوْ رِقٍّ. وَتُقْتَلُ الْجَمَاعَةُ بِالْوَاحِدِ.

There are four conditions for reciprocal killing [*qiṣāṣ*]:

a. the killer is mature and of sound mind;
b. the killer is not the victim's parent [or grandparent]; and
c. the victim is not lesser than the killer through unbelief or slavery.

A group is executed for killing an individual.

10.1.2 Non-Fatal Personal Injuries

وَكُلُّ شَخْصَيْنِ جَرَى الْقِصَاصُ بَيْنَهُمَا فِي النَّفْسِ يَجْرِي بَيْنَهُمَا فِي الْأَطْرَافِ.

وَشَرَائِطُ وُجُوبِ الْقِصَاصِ فِي الْأَطْرَافِ بَعْدَ الشَّرَائِطِ الْمَذْكُورَةِ اثْنَانِ: الِاشْتِرَاكُ فِي الِاسْمِ الْخَاصِّ: الْيُمْنَى بِالْيُمْنَى وَالْيُسْرَى بِالْيُسْرَى، وَأَنْ لَا يَكُونَ بِأَحَدِ الطَّرَفَيْنِ شَلَلٌ. وَكُلُّ عُضْوٍ أُخِذَ مِنْ مِفْصَلٍ فَفِيهِ الْقِصَاصُ. وَلَا قِصَاصَ فِي الْجُرُوحِ إِلَّا فِي الْمُوضِحَةِ.

When the rules of reciprocal punishment are applicable between two individuals, they also apply to non-fatal personal injuries.

The conditions for reciprocity being obligatory for non-fatal personal injuries, in addition to the previous conditions, are two:

a. sharing the specific name [with the severed part]: the right for the right, the left for the left; and
b. that one of the sides [of a pair] is not paralyzed.

Every limb that is taken from the joint is subject to reciprocity.

Wounds are not subject to reciprocity unless the injury cleaves flesh from the bone.

10.2 *Blood Indemnity*

(فَصْلٌ) وَالدِيَةُ عَلَى ضَرْبَيْنِ: مُغَلَّظَةٌ وَمُخَفَّفَةٌ.

There are two types of blood indemnity:

1. augmented; and
2. reduced.

10.2.1 Augmented

فَالْمُغَلَّظَةُ: مِائَةٌ مِنْ الْإِبِلِ: ثَلَاثُونَ حِقَّةً، وَثَلَاثُونَ جَذَعَةً، وَأَرْبَعُونَ خَلِفَةً فِي بُطُونِهَا أَوْلَادُهَا.

The augmented indemnity consists of 100 camels:[1]

a. 30 *ḥiqqah*;
b. 30 *jadha'ah*; and
c. 40 pregnant camels.

---

1 See "4.2 Camels" on page 47.

10.2.2 Reduced

وَالْمُخَفَّفَةُ: مِائَةٌ مِنْ الْإِبِلِ: عِشْرُونَ حِقَّةً، وَعِشْرُونَ جَذَعَةً، وَعِشْرُونَ بِنْتَ لَبُونٍ، وَعِشْرُونَ بِنْتَ مَخَاضٍ، وَعِشْرُونَ ابْنَ لَبُونٍ. فَإِنْ عُدِمَتْ الْإِبِلُ انْتَقَلَ إِلَى قِيمَتِهَا، وَقِيلَ: يَنْتَقِلُ إِلَى أَلْفِ دِينَارٍ، أَوْ إِلَى اثْنَيْ عَشَرَ أَلْفَ دِرْهَمٍ. وَإِنْ غُلِّظَتْ زِيدَ عَلَيْهَا الثُّلُثُ.

وَتُغَلَّظُ دِيَةُ الْخَطَأِ فِي ثَلَاثَةِ مَوَاضِعَ: إِذَا قَتَلَ فِي الْحَرَمِ، أَوْ فِي الْأَشْهُرِ الْحُرُمِ، أَوْ قَتَلَ ذَا رَحِمٍ مَحْرَمٍ.

وَدِيَةُ الْمَرْأَةِ عَلَى النِّصْفِ مِنْ دِيَةِ الرَّجُلِ، وَدِيَةُ الْيَهُودِيِّ وَالنَّصْرَانِيِّ ثُلُثُ دِيَةِ الْمُسْلِمِ، وأما دِيَةُ الْمَجُوسِيِّ ففيه ثُلُثَا عُشْرِ دِيَةِ الْمُسْلِمِ.

وَتَكْمُلُ دِيَةُ النَّفْسِ فِي الْيَدَيْنِ وَالرِّجْلَيْنِ وَالْأَنْفِ وَالْأُذُنَيْنِ وَالْعَيْنَيْنِ وَالْجُفُونِ الْأَرْبَعَةِ وَاللِّسَانِ وَالشَّفَتَيْنِ وَذَهَابِ الْكَلَامِ وَذَهَابِ الْبَصَرِ وَذَهَابِ السَّمْعِ وَذَهَابِ الشَّمِّ وَذَهَابِ الْعَقْلِ وَالذَّكَرِ وَالْأُنْثَيَيْنِ. وَفِي الْمُوضِحَةِ وَفِي السِّنِّ خَمْسٌ مِنْ الْإِبِلِ. وَفِي كُلِّ عُضْوٍ لَا مَنْفَعَةَ فِيهِ حُكُومَةٌ.

وَدِيَةُ الْعَبْدِ قِيمَتُهُ. وَدِيَةُ الْجَنِينِ الْحُرِّ غُرَّةٌ وَدِيَةُ الْجَنِينِ الْمَمْلُوكِ عُشْرُ قِيمَةِ أُمِّهِ.

The reduced indemnity consists of 100 camels:

a. 20 *hiqqah*;
b. 20 *jadha'ah*;
c. 20 *bint labūn*;
d. 20 *ibn labūn*; and
e. 20 *bint makhāḍ*.

If camels are absent, their value is used. It is also said that this is equivalent to 1 000 *dīnār* or 12 000 *dirham*; and one-third is added if the indemnity is augmented.

The indemnity for a mistaken killing is augmented in three contexts. [When one kills:]

1. within the Sacred Precinct;
2. during the Sacred Months;[2] or
3. one's close kin.

The indemnity for:

1. *a woman*: is half that of a male;
2. *a Jew or Christian*: is one-third that of a Muslim;
3. *a Zoroastrian*: is three-tenths that of a Muslim.

The indemnity is complete by loss of:

1. two hands;
2. two legs;
3. the nose;
4. two ears;
5. two eyes;
6. four eye lids;
7. the tongue;
8. two lips;
9. speech;
10. eyesight;
11. hearing;
12. smell;
13. soundness of mind;
14. the penis; and
15. two testicles.

2 The Sacred Months are Dhi al-Qa'dah, Dhi al-Ḥijjah, al-Maḥarram, and Rajab.

Five camels are owed for a wound that cleaves flesh from the bone; and for each tooth.

A judgment is made for each limb that does not have a particular use [e.g., a paralyzed limb; a man's nipples].[3]

The indemnity for [killing] a slave is the slave's value.

The indemnity for causing a free woman to miscarry is a male or female slave.[4] The indemnity for causing a slave to miscarry is one-tenth the mother's value.

10.3 *Allegations*

(فَصْلٌ) وَإِذَا اقْتَرَنَ بِدَعْوَى الدَّمِ لَوْثٌ يَقَعُ بِهِ فِي النَّفْسِ صِدْقُ الْمُدَّعِي حَلَفَ الْمُدَّعِي خَمْسِينَ يَمِينًا وَاسْتَحَقَّ الدِّيَةَ، وَإِنْ لَمْ يَكُنْ هُنَاكَ لَوْثٌ فَالْيَمِينُ عَلَى الْمُدَّعَى عَلَيْهِ.

If one of the victim's survivors presents an allegation accompanied by corroborating evidence that convinces one that the claim is true, the survivor swears an oath 50 times and the indemnity becomes due. When corroborating evidence is absent, the defendant swears [that the allegation is false].

10.4 *Expiation*

وَعَلَى قَاتِلِ النَّفْسِ الْمُحَرَّمَةِ كَفَّارَةٌ: عِتْقُ رَقَبَةٍ مُؤْمِنَةٍ سَلِيمَةٍ مِنَ الْعُيُوبِ الْمُضِرَّةِ، فَإِنْ لَمْ يَجِدْ فَصِيَامُ شَهْرَيْنِ مُتَتَابِعَيْنِ.

3 The judgment is made by determining how much such an injury reduces a slave's price.

4 The value of the slave must be at least one-twentieth the value of an indemnity.

When the killer has killed someone whose life is sacrosanct,[5] he must make an expiation by manumitting a Muslim slave who is free of defects [which would prevent the slave from working]. If no such slave is found, one fasts two months consecutively.

5 All life is sacrosanct except for non-Muslims at war with Muslims, apostates, adulterers the court has sentenced to death by lapidation and those obligatory to kill by military action.

11

PUNISHMENTS

كِتَابُ الْحُدُودِ

11.1 *Fornication*

وَالزَّانِي عَلَى ضَرْبَيْنِ: مُحْصَنٍ، وَغَيْرِ مُحْصَنٍ. فَالْمُحْصَنُ حَدُّهُ الرَّجْمُ وَغَيْرُ الْمُحْصَنِ حَدُّهُ مِائَةُ جَلْدَةٍ وَتَغْرِيبُ عَامٍ إِلَى مَسَافَةِ الْقَصْرِ.

There are two types of fornicators:

1. those who have the capacity to remain chaste;
2. those who do not.

The penalty for those who have the capacity to remain chaste is lapidation [until death].

For others, the penalty is a flogging of 100 lashes, and banishment for one year to [at least] the distance for shortening prayers.

11.1.1 The Capacity to Remain Chaste

وَشَرَائِطُ الْإِحْصَانِ أَرْبَعَةٌ: الْبُلُوغُ، وَالْعَقْلُ، وَالْحُرِّيَّةُ، وَوُجُودُ الْوَطْءِ فِي نِكَاحٍ صَحِيحٍ. وَالْعَبْدُ وَالْأَمَةُ حَدُّهُمَا نِصْفُ حَدِّ الْحُرِّ.

There are four conditions for the capacity to remain chaste [*muḥsin*]. [One must:]

a. be mature;
b. be of sound mind;
c. be free; and
d. have had intercourse within a valid marriage.

The punishment for male and female slaves is half the punishment of non-slaves.[1]

11.1.2 Sodomy and Bestiality

وَحُكْمُ اللِّوَاطِ وَإِتْيَانِ الْبَهَائِمِ كَحُكْمِ الزِّنَا.

The punishment for [performing] sodomy and bestiality is the same as for fornication.[2]

11.1.3 Intimate Contact

وَمَنْ وَطِئَ فِيمَا دُونَ الْفَرْجِ عُزِّرَ. ولا يَبْلُغُ بِالتَّعْزِيرِ أَدْنَى الْحُدُودِ.

Someone who has intimate contact other than genital penetration is subject to a discretionary punishment [*ta'zīr*] that is less than the lowest of the set punishments [i.e., 40 lashes].

11.2 Accusing a Person of Fornication

(فَصْلٌ) وَإِذَا قَذَفَ غَيْرَهُ بِالزِّنَا فَعَلَيْهِ حَدُّ الْقَذْفِ بثَمَانِيَةِ شَرَائِطَ. ثَلاثَةٌ مِنْهَا فِي الْقَاذِفِ، وَهُوَ: أَنْ يَكُونَ بَالِغًا، عَاقِلًا، وَأَنْ لَا يَكُونَ وَالِدًا لِلْمَقْذُوفِ. وَخَمْسَةٌ

1 Since slaves do not meet the conditions for being chaste, lapidation is *never* a possible punishment.

2 The active participant in sodomy is punished as stated unless it was performed with one's wife, in which case there is a discretionary punishment [*ta'zīr*]. Otherwise, the passive participant is given 100 lashes and banished for one year. Someone who commits bestiality is given a discretionary punishment.

فِي المَقْذُوفِ، وَهُوَ: أَنْ يَكُونَ مُسْلِمًا، بَالِغًا، عَاقِلًا، حُرًّا، عَفِيفًا. وَيُحَدُّ الحُرُّ ثَمَانِينَ، وَالعَبْدُ أَرْبَعِينَ.

وَيَسْقُطُ حَدُّ الْقَذْفِ بِثَلَاثَةِ أَشْيَاءَ: إِقَامَةُ الْبَيِّنَةِ، أَوْ عَفْوُ المَقْذُوفِ، أَوْ اللِّعَانُ فِي حَقِّ الزَّوْجَةِ.

When one accuses another person of fornication, there is an obligatory punishment for the accusation if eight conditions are met.

Three conditions concern the accuser. [The accuser must:]

a. be mature;
b. be of sound mind; and
c. not be a parent of the accused.

Five conditions concern the accused. [The accused must be:]

a. a Muslim;
b. mature;
c. of sound mind;
d. free; and
e. chaste.

A free person is flogged 80 lashes; a slave is flogged 40.

The punishment for an accusation of fornication is dropped provided [one of] three conditions are met:

a. proof is brought;[3]
b. the accused pardons them; or
c. public imprecation[4] when made against one's wife.

3 See "16.3 Evidence" on page 152.
4 See "9.11 Charging One's Wife With Adultery" on page 110.

11.3 *Alcohol and Liquid Intoxicants*

(فَصْلٌ) وَمَنْ شَرِبَ خَمْرًا أَوْ شَرَابًا مُسْكِرًا يُحَدُّ أَرْبَعِينَ، وَيَجُوزُ أَنْ يَبْلُغَ بِهِ ثَمَانِينَ عَلَى وَجْهِ التَّعْزِيرِ. وَيَجِبُ عَلَيْهِ الْحَدُّ بِأَحَدِ أَمْرَيْنِ: بِالْبَيِّنَةِ أَوْ الْإِقْرَارِ، وَلَا يُحَدُّ بالقَيْءِ والاِستِنكَاهِ.

Anyone who drinks alcohol or liquid intoxicants is flogged 40 lashes. At the [judge's] discretion, it is permissible for the punishment to reach 80 lashes.

The punishment becomes obligatory through one of two means:

1. evidence;[5] or
2. an admission.[6]

It does not become obligatory because of vomit or [the] smell [of alcohol].

11.4 *Burglary*

(فَصْلٌ) وتُقْطَعُ يدُ السَّارِقِ بِثَلَاثَةِ شَرَائِطَ: أَنْ يَكُونَ بَالِغًا، عَاقِلًا، وَأَنْ يَسْرِقَ نِصَابًا قِيمَتُهُ رُبُعُ دِينَارٍ مِنْ حِرْزِ مِثْلِهِ، لَا مِلْكَ لَهُ فِيهِ وَلَا شُبْهَةَ لَهُ فِي مَالِ الْمَسْرُوقِ مِنْهُ.

وَتُقْطَعُ يَدُهُ الْيُمْنَى مِنْ مَفْصِلِ الْكُوعِ، فَإِنْ سَرَقَ ثَانِيًا قُطِعَتْ رِجْلُهُ الْيُسْرَى، فَإِنْ سَرَقَ ثَالِثًا قُطِعَتْ يَدُهُ الْيُسْرَى، فَإِنْ سَرَقَ رَابِعًا قُطِعَتْ رِجْلُهُ الْيُمْنَى، فَإِنْ سَرَقَ بَعْدَ ذَلِكَ عُزِّرَ وَقِيلَ: يُقْتَلُ صَبْرًا.

---

5 See "16.3 Evidence" on page 152.
6 See "7.14 Admissions" on page 75.

A burglar's hand is amputated provided three conditions are met. [The burglar must:]

a. be mature;
b. be of sound mind; and,
c. an item with a value that exceeds one-quarter *dinār*,[7] [taken] from a place that affords the security typical for safeguarding such items, and in which he does not have co-ownership nor some relationship with the owner.

The right hand is amputated at the wrist. If one then steals a second time, the left foot is amputated. If one steals a third time, the left hand is amputated. If one steals a fourth time, the right foot is amputated. If one steals after this, one is given a discretionary punishment; according to another opinion he is executed.

11.5 *Highway Robbery*

(فَصْلٌ) وَقُطَّاعُ الطَّرِيقِ عَلَى أَرْبَعَةِ أَقْسَامٍ: إِنْ قَتَلُوا وَلَمْ يَأْخُذُوا المَالَ قُتِلُوا، فَإِنْ قَتَلُوا وَأَخَذُوا المَالَ قُتِلُوا وَصُلِبُوا، فَإِنْ أَخَذُوا المَالَ وَلَمْ يَقْتُلُوا قُطِعَتْ أَيْدِيهِمْ وَأَرْجُلُهُمْ مِنْ خِلَافٍ، فَإِنْ أَخَافُوا السَّبِيلَ وَلَمْ يَأْخُذُوا مَالًا وَلَمْ يَقْتُلُوا حُبِسُوا وَعُزِّرُوا. وَمَنْ تَابَ مِنْهُمْ قَبْلَ القُدرَةِ عَلَيْهِ سَقَطَتْ عَنْهُ الحُدُودُ وَأُخِذَ بِالحُقُوقِ.

There are four types of highway robbers.

1. If they *kill but do not steal*: they are executed.
2. If they *kill and steal*: they are executed and crucified.
3. If they *steal but do not kill*: their right hand and left foot are amputated.
4. If they *spread fear along the highway without stealing anything*: they are not executed, but they are imprisoned and given a discretionary punishment.

---

7 One-quarter of a *dinār* is 1.058 grams of pure gold.

If any of them repents before being apprehended, the mandatory amputation, execution and crucifixion are dropped, though they are still liable for personal injuries, theft and other crimes against their victims.

11.6 *Self-Defense*

(فَصْلٌ) وَمَنْ قُصِدَ بِأَذًى فِي نَفْسِهِ أَوْ مَالِهِ أَوْ حَرِيمِهِ فَقَاتَلَ عَنْ ذَلِكَ وَقَتَلَ فَلَا ضَمَانَ عَلَيْهِ.

One is not held liable if one kills in the process of resisting harm aimed at one's person, property or those for whom one is responsible.

11.6.1 Animals

وَعَلَى رَاكِبِ الدَّابَّةِ ضَمَانُ مَا أَتْلَفَتْهُ دَابَّتُهُ.

An animal's rider is liable for what the animal destroys.

11.7 *Renegades*

(فَصْلٌ) وَيُقَاتَلُ أَهْلُ الْبَغْيِ بِثَلَاثَةِ شَرَائِطَ: أَنْ يَكُونُوا فِي مَنَعَةٍ، وَأَنْ يَخْرُجُوا عَنْ قَبْضَةِ الْإِمَامِ، وَأَنْ يَكُونَ لَهُمْ تَأْوِيلٌ سَائِغٌ. وَلَا يُقْتَلُ أَسِيرُهُمْ، وَلَا يُغْنَمُ مَالُهُمْ، وَلَا يُذَفَّفُ عَلَى جَرِيحِهِمْ.

Fighting those who rebel against the Imam is obligatory when three conditions are met. [That the group:]

a. poses a true physical threat;
b. has removed themselves from obeying the Imam; and
c. possesses a reasonable explanation [for disobeying the Imam].

If rebels are taken as prisoners of war, they are not executed. Their property is not taken as spoils of war and their wounded are not executed.

11.8 Apostasy

(فَصْلٌ) وَمَنِ ارْتَدَّ عَنْ الْإِسْلَامِ اُسْتُتِيبَ ثَلَاثًا، فَإِنْ تَابَ وَإِلَّا قُتِلَ. وَلَمْ يُغَسَّلْ، وَلَمْ يُصَلَّ عَلَيْهِ وَلَمْ يُدْفَنْ فِي مَقَابِرِ الْمُسْلِمِينَ.

An apostate is given three opportunities to repent. If he does not repent, he is executed; he is not washed, prayed over or buried among the Muslims.

11.9 Omitting Prayer

(فَصْلٌ) وَتَارِكُ الصَّلَاةِ عَلَى ضَرْبَيْنِ؛ أَحَدُهُمَا: أَنْ يَتْرُكَهَا غَيْرَ مُعْتَقِدٍ لِوُجُوبِهَا، فَحُكْمُهُ حُكْمُ الْمُرْتَدِّ. وَالثَّانِي: أَنْ يَتْرُكَهَا كَسَلًا مُعْتَقِدًا لِوُجُوبِهَا فَيُسْتَتَابُ، فَإِنْ تَابَ وَصَلَّى وَإِلَّا قُتِلَ بِالسَّيْفِ حَدًّا، وَحُكْمُهُ حُكْمُ الْمُسْلِمِينَ.

There are two categories of people who omit prayer. Those who omit prayer:

1. *because they do not consider it obligatory*: their ruling is the same as that for apostates.
2. *out of laziness, while believing that it is obligatory*: they are given the opportunity to repent. If they do not repent *and* perform the prayer, they are executed as punishment while their ruling is that of Muslims.

12

JIHAD

كِتَابُ الجِهَادِ

12.1 *Obligatory Jihad*

وَشَرَائِطُ وُجُوبِ الْجِهَادِ سَبْعُ خِصَالٍ: الْإِسْلَامُ، وَالْبُلُوغُ، وَالْعقْلُ، وَالْحُرِّيَّةُ، وَالذُّكُورَةُ، وَالصِّحَّةُ، وَالطَّاقَةُ عَلَى الْقِتَالِ.

There are seven conditions obligating jihad. [The person must be:]

a. a Muslim;
b. mature;
c. of sound mind;
d. free;
e. male;
f. healthy; and
g. able to fight.

12.1.1 Prisoners

وَمَنْ أُسِرَ مِنْ الْكُفَّارِ فَعَلَى ضَرْبَيْنِ: ضَرْبٍ يَكُونُ رَقِيقًا بِنَفْسِ السَّبْيِ وَهُمُ النِّسَاءُ وَالصِّبْيَانُ. وَضَرْبٍ لَا يرِقُّ بِنَفْسِ السَّبْيِ وَهُمُ الرِّجَالُ البَالِغُونَ، وَالْإِمَامُ مُخَيَّرٌ فِيهِمْ بَيْنَ أَرْبَعَةِ أَشْيَاءَ: الْقَتْلُ، وَالِاسْتِرْقَاقُ، وَالْمَنُّ، وَالْفِدْيَةُ بِالْمَالِ أَوْ بِالرِّجَالِ؛ يَفْعَلُ الْإِمَامُ مَا فِيهِ الْمَصْلَحَةُ. وَمَنْ أَسْلَمَ قَبْلَ الْأَسْرِ أَحْرَزَ مَالَهُ وَدَمَهُ وَصِغَارَ أَوْلَادِهِ.

وَيُحْكَمُ لِلصَّبِيِّ بِالْإِسْلَامِ عِنْدَ وُجُودِ ثَلَاثَةِ أَسْبَابٍ: أَنْ يُسْلِمَ أَحَدُ أَبَوَيْهِ، أَوْ يَسْبِيَهُ مُسْلِمٌ مُنْفَرِدًا عَنْ أَبَوَيْهِ، أَوْ يُوجَدُ لَقِيطًا فِي دَارِ الْإِسْلَامِ.

There are two types of captured disbelievers:

1. *Automatically enslaved by capture*: they are females and young males.
2. *Not automatically enslaved by capture*: they are mature males. The Imam chooses whichever of four things is best [for the community]:
   a. execution;
   b. slavery;
   c. freeing them; or
   d. ransoming them for money or captives.

Whoever enters Islam before capture, his property, life and young children are protected.

A child is judged to be Muslim when [one of] three causes [exists]:

1. one of the parents [or grandparents] enters Islam;
2. a Muslim takes the child captive independently of the parents; or
3. the child is found within Muslim lands.

12.2 *Spoils of War*

(فَصْلٌ) وَمَنْ قَتَلَ قَتِيلًا أُعْطِيَ سَلَبَهُ، وَتُقْسَمُ الْغَنِيمَةُ بَعْدَ ذَلِكَ على خَمْسَةِ أَخْمَاسٍ، فَيُعْطَى أَرْبَعَةُ أَخْمَاسِهَا لِمَنْ شَهِدَ الْوَقْعَةَ، وَيُعْطَى لِلْفَارِسِ ثَلَاثَةُ أَسْهُمٍ، وَلِلرَّاجِلِ سَهْمٌ.

وَلَا يُسْهَمُ إِلَّا لِمَنْ اُسْتُكْمِلَتْ فِيهِ خَمْسُ شَرَائِطَ: الْإِسْلَامُ، وَالْبُلُوغُ، وَالْعَقْلُ، وَالْحُرِّيَّةُ، وَالذُّكُورَةُ. فَإِنْ اخْتَلَّ شَرْطٌ مِنْ ذَلِكَ رُضِخَ لَهُ وَلَمْ يُسْهَمْ لَهُ.

وَيُقْسَمُ الْخُمُسَ عَلَى خَمْسَةِ أَسْهُمٍ: سَهْمٌ لِرَسُولِ اللهِ - صَلَّى اللهُ عَلَيْهِ وَسَلَّمَ - يُصْرَفُ بَعْدَهُ لِلْمَصَالِحِ، وَسَهْمٌ لِذَوِي الْقُرْبَى وَهُمْ: بَنُو هَاشِمٍ وَبَنُو الْمُطَّلِبِ، وَسَهْمٌ لِلْيَتَامَى، وَسَهْمٌ لِلْمَسَاكِينِ، وَسَهْمٌ لِابْنِ السَّبِيلِ.

Whoever kills [or disables] an enemy is given his personal belongings. After this [is taken care of], the spoils are distributed in five-fifths:

1. Four-fifths are given to those who participated in the battle.

   Cavalry receive three shares;[1] foot soldiers receive one.

   Shares are given only to those who fulfill five conditions. [The recipient must be:]

   a. a Muslim;
   b. mature;
   c. of sound mind;
   d. free; and
   e. male.

   If one of these conditions is missing, the person is given a token payment at the Imam's discretion.

2. One-fifth is divided into five shares:

   a. one for the Prophet ﷺ; after him ﷺ, it is distributed for the public welfare;
   b. one for the relatives of the Prophet ﷺ from Banī Hāshim and Banī al-Muṭṭalib;
   c. one for orphans;
   d. one for wayfarers.

1 Two shares are for the horse's owner; one for the rider.

12.3 *Tribute*

(فَصْلٌ) وَيُقْسَمُ مَالُ الْفَيْءِ عَلَى خَمْسِ فِرَقٍ: يُصْرَفُ خُمُسُهُ عَلَى مَنْ يُصْرَفُ عَلَيْهِمْ خُمُسُ الْغَنِيمَةِ، وَيُعْطَى أَرْبَعَةُ أَخْمَاسِهَا لِلْمُقَاتِلَةِ وَفِي مَصَالِحِ الْمُسْلِمِينَ.

The tribute [Ar. *fay'*] is divided into five parts:

1. one-fifth is given to those who receive one-fifth from the spoils of war; and
2. four-fifths are given for [the needs of] soldiers and for the public welfare.

12.4 *Non-Muslim Subjects of the Islamic State*

(فَصْلٌ) وَشَرَائِطُ وُجُوبِ الْجِزْيَةِ خَمْسُ خِصَالٍ: الْبُلُوغُ، وَالْعَقْلُ، وَالْحُرِّيَّةُ، وَالذُّكُورِيَّةُ، وَأَنْ يَكُونَ مِنْ أَهْلِ الْكِتَابِ أَوْ مِمَّنْ لَهُ شُبْهَةُ كِتَابٍ.

وَأَقَلُّ الْجِزْيَةِ دِينَارٌ فِي كُلِّ حَوْلٍ. وَيُؤْخَذُ مِنَ الْمُتَوَسِّطِ دِينَارَانِ، وَمِنَ الْمُوسِرِ أَرْبَعَةُ دَنَانِيرَ. وَيَجُوزُ أَنْ يَشْتَرِطَ عَلَيْهِمُ الضِّيَافَةَ فَضْلًا عَنْ مِقْدَارِ الْجِزْيَةِ.

There are five conditions which make the *jizyah* [non-Muslim poll tax] obligatory. [The person paying it must be:]

a. mature;
b. of sound mind;
c. free;
d. male;
e. a member of the People of the Book or those who have something that could be revelation.[2]

2 A condition for something that could be revelation is that it predates Islam.

The minimum amount for the *jizyah* is one *dīnār* [4.235 grams of pure gold] yearly; two *dīnār*s are taken from the "middle class;" and four from the affluent.[3]

It is permissible to stipulate that they accommodate travelers in addition to the *jizyah*.

12.4.1 The Contract With Non-Muslim Subjects

وَيَتَضَمَّنُ عَقْدُ الذِّمَّةِ أَرْبَعَةَ أَشْيَاءَ: أَنْ يُؤَدُّوا الْجِزْيَةَ، وَأَنْ تَجْرِيَ عَلَيْهِمْ أَحْكَامُ الْإِسْلَامِ، وَأَنْ لَا يَذْكُرُوا دِينَ الْإِسْلَامِ إِلَّا بِخَيْرٍ، وَأَنْ لَا يَفْعَلُوا مَا فِيهِ ضَرَرٌ عَلَى الْمُسْلِمِينَ. وَيُعْرَفُونَ بِلُبْسِ الْغِيَارِ وَشَدِّ الزُّنَّارِ، وَيُمْنَعُونَ مِنْ رُكُوبِ الْخَيْلِ.

The contract with non-Muslim subjects consists of four things. [The non-Muslim subject must:]

a. pay the *jizyah*;
b. comply with Islamic Law;[4]
c. mention only good things about Islam; and
d. not do anything that harms Muslims.

[Non-Muslim subjects] are identified by wearing distinctive clothing and a [colored] sash, and they are prevented from riding horses.

3 The amounts, on 18 May 2013, were approximately USD $202, $405, and $810. Please see http://www.e-nisab.com/misc for current values.

4 They are required to avoid things both religions consider unlawful, including theft, murder and fornication.

13

HUNTING AND SLAUGHTERING

كِتَابُ الصَّيْدِ وَالْذَّبَائِحِ

13.1 *Slaughtering*

وَمَا قُدِرَ عَلَى ذَكَاتِهِ فَذَكَاتُهُ فِي حَلْقِهِ وَلَبَّتِهِ، وَمَا لَمْ يُقْدَرْ عَلَى ذَكَاتِهِ فَذَكَاتُهُ عَقْرُهُ حَيْثُ قُدِرَ عَلَيْهِ. وَكَمَالُ الذَّكَاةِ أَرْبَعَةُ أَشْيَاءَ: قَطْعُ الْحُلْقُومِ، وَالْمَرِيءِ، وَالْوَدَجَيْنِ. وَالْمُجْزِئُ مِنْهَا شَيْئَانِ: قَطْعُ الْحُلْقُومِ، وَالْمَرِيءِ.

When possible, an animal is slaughtered by cutting its throat or at the base of the neck.

An animal which it is not possible to slaughter [as mentioned above], is slaughtered by wounding it however one can [until it dies].

The complete [way of] slaughtering is to cut four things:

1. the throat;
2. the esophagus; and

3–4. both jugular veins.

What suffices is [cutting] two things:

a. the throat; and
b. the esophagus.

13.1.1 Hunting

وَيَجُوزُ الاِصْطِيَادُ بِكُلِّ جَارِحَةٍ مُعَلَّمَةٍ مِنَ السِّبَاعِ وَمِنْ جَوَارِحِ الطَّيْرِ. وَشَرَائِطُ تَعْلِيمِهَا أَرْبَعَةٌ: أَنْ تَكُونَ إِذَا أُرْسِلَتْ اسْتَرْسَلَتْ، وَإِذَا زُجِرَتْ انْزَجَرَتْ، وَإِذَا قَتَلَتْ صَيْدًا لَمْ تَأْكُلْ مِنْهُ شَيْئًا، وَأَنْ يَتَكَرَّرَ ذَلِكَ مِنْهَا. فَإِنْ عُدِمَ أَحَدُ هَذِهِ الشُّرُوطِ لَمْ يَحِلَّ مَا أَخَذَتْهُ إِلَّا أَنْ يُدْرَكَ حَيًّا فَيُذَكَّى.

It is permissible to hunt using all types of trained, predatory land animals and predatory birds.

There are four conditions for the animal being trained:

a. when it is sent, it goes;
b. when it is told to stop, it stops;
c. if it kills the prey, it eats nothing from it; and
d. it does the above repeatedly.

If one of the above conditions is missing, its prey is not permissible [to eat], unless it is still alive [when the human takes it] and it is slaughtered.

13.1.2 The Implement

وَتَجُوزُ الذَّكَاةُ بِكُلِّ مَا يَجْرَحُ إِلَّا بِالسِّنِّ وَالظُّفْرِ.

It is permissible to slaughter using any implement that draws blood, except for teeth and fingernails.

13.1.3 Various Rulings

وَتَحِلُّ ذَكَاةُ كُلِّ مُسْلِمٍ وَكِتَابِيٍّ، وَلَا تَحِلُّ ذَكَاةُ مَجُوسِيٍّ وَلَا وَثَنِيٍّ. وَذَكَاةُ الْجَنِينِ بِذَكَاةِ أُمِّهِ، إِلَّا أَنْ يُوجَدَ حَيًّا فَيُذَكَّى. وَمَا قُطِعَ مِنْ حَيٍّ فَهُوَ مَيِّتٌ إِلَّا الشُّعُورَ الْمُنْتَفَعَ بِهَا فِي الْمَفَارِشِ وَالْمَلَابِسِ.

Animals slaughtered by all Muslims and People of the Book are lawful. Slaughtering performed by Zoroastrian and idolaters is unlawful.

An unborn animal is slaughtered by slaughtering its mother, unless it remains alive. In that case, it, too, is slaughtered.

Whatever is severed from a living animal is the same as if it came from the animal without it being [properly] slaughtered,[1] except for hair [from an edible animal] which can be used for bedding and clothes.

13.2 *Different Types of Foods*

(فَصْلٌ) وَكُلُّ حَيَوانٍ اسْتَطَابَتْهُ الْعَرَبُ فَهُوَ حَلَالٌ إِلَّا مَا وَرَدَ الشَّرْعُ بِتَحْرِيمِهِ. وَكُلُّ حَيَوانٍ اسْتَخْبَثَتْهُ لْعَرَبُ فَهُوَ حَرَامٌ إِلَّا مَا وَرَدَ الشَّرْعُ بِإِبَاحَتِهِ.

وَيَحْرُمُ مِنْ السِّبَاعِ مَا لَهُ نَابٌ قَوِيٌّ يَعْدُو بِهِ، وَيَحْرُمُ مِنْ الطُّيُورِ مَا لَهُ مِخْلَبٌ قَوِيٌّ يَجْرَحُ بِهِ.

وَيَحِلُّ لِلْمُضْطَرِّ فِي الْمَخْمَصَةِ أَنْ يَأْكُلَ مِنْ الْمَيْتَةِ الْمُحَرَّمَةِ مَا يَسُدُّ بِهِ رَمَقَهُ.

وَلَنَا مَيْتَتَانِ حَلَالَانِ: السَّمَكُ وَالْجَرَادُ، وَدَمَانِ حَلَالَانِ: الْكَبِدُ وَالطِّحَالُ.

---

1 Thus, something severed from a living animal is filth.

Everything edible that the Arabs [during the Prophet's time ﷺ] considered wholesome is lawful, except for things that the Shāri'ah specifically declares unlawful.

Everything edible that the Arabs [during the Prophet's time ﷺ] considered disgusting is unlawful, except for those things the Shāri'ah specifically declares lawful.

Predatory land animals that have strong fangs used for injuring [prey] are unlawful.

Predatory birds that have strong talons used for wounding are unlawful.

It is permissible for someone on the verge of starvation to consume meat from an animal that has not been [properly] slaughtered—and is unlawful [to consume]—to the extent necessary to preserve life.

Two types of unslaughtered flesh are lawful for us:

1. fish; and
2. locusts.

Two types of blood are lawful for us:

1. liver; and
2. spleen.

13.3 Offering Sacrifices

(فَصْلٌ) والأُضْحِيَةُ سُنَّةٌ مُؤَكَّدَةٌ. وَيُجْزِئُ فِيهَا الْجَذَعُ مِنَ الضَّأْنِ، وَالثَّنِيُّ مِنَ الْمَعْزِ، وَالثَّنِيُّ مِنَ الْإِبِلِ، وَالثَّنِيُّ مِنَ الْبَقَرِ.

وَتُجْزِئُ الْبَدَنَةُ عَنْ سَبْعَةٍ، وَالْبَقَرَةُ عَنْ سَبْعَةٍ، وَالشَّاةُ عَنْ وَاحِدٍ.

Offering an animal sacrifice [*aḍḥiyah*] is an emphasized sunnah.

The following suffice [for sacrifices]:

1. a one-year old male sheep;
2. a two-year-old male goat;
3. a five-year-old camel; and
4. a two-year-old cow.

One adult camel suffices for seven [individual sacrifices].

One [adult] cow suffices for seven.

One female sheep suffices for an individual.

13.3.1 Defective Animals

وَأَرْبَعٌ لَا تُجْزِئُ فِي الضَّحَايَا: الْعَوْرَاءُ الْبَيِّنُ عَوَرُهَا، وَالْعَرْجَاءُ الْبَيِّنُ عَرَجُهَا، وَالْمَرِيضَةُ الْبَيِّنُ مَرَضُهَا، وَالْعَجْفَاءُ الَّتِي ذَهَبَ مُخُّهَا مِنَ الْهُزَالِ. وَيُجْزِئُ الْخَصِيُّ، وَالْمَكْسُورُ الْقَرْنِ. وَلَا يُجْزِئُ مَقْطُوعَةُ الْأُذُنِ وَالذَّنَبِ.

The following defects render the animal insufficient as a sacrifice. [When the animal:]

1. has obvious blindness;
2. is obviously lame;
3. is obviously sick; or
4. is so sick that it is senseless.

An animal that is castrated or has a broken horn suffices.

An animal whose ear or tail has been cut does not suffice.

13.3.2 Time

وَوَقْتُ الذَّبْحِ مِنْ وَقْتِ صَلَاةِ الْعِيدِ إِلَى غُرُوبِ الشَّمْسِ مِنْ آخِرِ أَيَّامِ التَّشْرِيقِ.

The time for the sacrifice begins at the time of the 'Eid Prayer and extends until sunset on the third day after 'Eid al-Aḍhā.[2]

13.3.3 Recommended Actions

وَيُسْتَحَبُّ عِنْدَ الذَّبْحِ خَمْسَةُ أَشْيَاءَ: التَّسْمِيَةُ، وَالصَّلَاةُ عَلَى رَسُولِ اللهِ - صَلَّى اللهُ عَلَيْهِ وَسَلَّمَ -، وَاسْتِقْبَالُ الْقِبْلَةِ بِالذَّبِيحَةِ، وَالتَّكْبِيرُ، وَالدُّعَاءُ بِالْقَبُولِ.

وَلَا يَأْكُلُ الْمُضَحِّي شَيْئًا مِنَ الْأُضْحِيَّةِ الْمَنْذُورَةِ، وَيَأْكُلُ مِنَ الْأُضْحِيَّةِ الْمُتَطَوَّعِ بِهَا، وَلَا يَبِيعُ مِنَ الْأُضْحِيَّةِ، وَيُطْعِمُ الْفُقَرَاءَ وَالْمَسَاكِينَ.

Five actions are recommended when slaughtering. [One should:]

1. say *bismillāh*;
2. offer prayers upon the Prophet ﷺ;
3. face the direction of prayer;
4. say *Allāhu akbar*; and
5. supplicate for its acceptance.

The person offering the sacrifice does not eat from a sacrifice he has sworn to perform [and thus made obligatory upon himself], though he can eat from a voluntary sacrifice.

No part of the sacrifice is to be sold. [The meat] is fed to the poor and destitute.

2 The relied-upon opinion is that the time begins when the sun rises and enough time has passed to pray two *rak'at* and deliver a short sermon.

13.4 *Slaughtering for a Newborn*

(فَصْلٌ) وَالْعَقِيقَةُ مُسْتَحَبَّةٌ، وَهِيَ الذَّبِيحة عَنِ الْمَوْلُوْدِ يَوْمَ سَابِعِهِ. وَيُذْبَحُ عَنْ الْغُلَامِ شَاتَانِ، وَعَنْ الْجَارِيَةِ شَاةٌ، وَيُطْعَمُ الْفُقَرَاءُ وَالْمَسَاكِينُ.

It is recommended to slaughter for a newborn on the seventh day after birth.

Two female sheep are slaughtered for a boy and one for a girl.

The meat is fed to the poor and destitute.

14

CONTESTS AND MARKSMANSHIP

كِتَابُ السَّبْقِ وَالرَّمِي

وَتَصِحُّ المُسَابَقَةُ عَلَى الدَّوَابِّ وَالمُنَاضَلَةُ بِالسِّهامِ إِذَا كَانَتْ المَسَافَةُ مَعْلُومَةً، وَصِفَةُ المُنَاضَلَةِ مَعْلُومَةً. وَيُخْرِجُ الْعِوَضَ أَحَدُ المُتَسَابِقَيْنِ حَتَّى إِذَا سَبَقَ اسْتَرَدَّهُ، وَإِنْ سُبِقَ أَخَذَهُ صَاحِبُهُ لَهُ. وَإِنْ أَخْرَجَاهُ مَعًا لَمْ يَجُزْ إِلَّا أَنْ يُدْخِلَا بَيْنَهُمَا مُحَلِّلًا، فَإِنْ سَبَقَ أَخَذَ العِوَضَ، وَإِنْ سُبِقَ لَمْ يَغْرَمْ.

Racing and marksmanship contests are permissible provided the distance and parameters for the marksmanship are defined.

The wager is taken from one of the participants, such that if he wins he takes it back and if he loses it is taken from him.

If both participants offer a wager, the contract is not permissible until an additional non-wagering participant [*muḥallil*] enters [the contest]. He takes the wager if he wins and he loses nothing if he does not.

15

OATHS AND VOWS

كِتَابُ الْأَيْمَانِ وَالنُّذُوْرِ

15.1 Oaths

وَلَا تَنْعَقِدُ الْيَمِينُ إِلَّا بِاللهِ تَعَالَى، أَوْ بِاسْمٍ مِنْ أَسْمَائِهِ، أَوْ صِفَةٍ مِنْ صِفَاتِ ذَاتِهِ. وَمَنْ حَلَفَ بِصَدَقَةِ مَالِهِ فَهُوَ مُخَيَّرٌ بَيْنَ الصَّدَقَةِ وَالْكَفَّارَةِ. وَلَا شَيْءَ فِي لَغْوِ الْيَمِينِ. وَمَنْ حَلَفَ أَنْ لَا يَفْعَلَ شَيْئًا فَأَمَرَ غَيْرَهُ بِفِعْلِهِ لَمْ يَحْنَثْ، وَمَنْ حَلَفَ عَلَى فِعْلِ أَمْرَيْنِ فَفَعَلَ أَحَدَهُمَا لَمْ يَحْنَثْ.

An oath [*yamīn*] does not become binding unless it includes mention of:

1. Allah Most High;
2. one of His names; or
3. one of His attributes.

Whoever vows to give his property as charity must choose between giving away all of his property, or making an expiation for breaking an oath.

No expiation is necessary for oaths made unthinkingly.

If one swears to abstain from something, he has not broken his oath if he performs something else.

If one swears to abstain from something, he has not broken his oath if he orders someone else to perform it.

If one swears to avoid two things, he has not broken his oath if he performs [just] one of them.

15.2 *The Expiation for Broken Oaths*

وَكَفَّارَةُ الْيَمِينِ هُوَ مُخَيَّرٌ فِيهَا بَيْنَ ثَلَاثَةِ أَشْيَاءَ: عِتْقُ رَقَبَةٍ مُؤْمِنَةٍ، أَوْ إِطْعَامُ عَشَرَةِ مَسَاكِينَ كُلُّ مِسْكِينٍ مُدًّا، أَوْ كِسْوَتُهُمْ ثَوْبًا ثَوْبًا. فَإِنْ لَمْ يَجِدْ فَصِيَامُ ثَلَاثَةِ أَيَّامٍ.

[To perform] the expiation for broken oaths, one chooses between three options:

1. manumission of a Muslim slave;
2. feeding ten of the poor: giving each one 0.51 liters [*mudd*] of food, or clothing each with a single article of clothing;

or, when one is incapable of the above,

3. fasting three days.

15.3 *Vows*

(فَصْلٌ) وَالنَّذْرُ يَلْزَمُ فِي الْمُجَازَاةِ عَلَى مُبَاحٍ وَطَاعَةٍ كَقَوْلِهِ: «إِنْ شَفَى اللهُ مَرِيضِي فَلِلَّهِ عَلَيَّ أَنْ أُصَلِّيَ» أَوْ «أَصُومَ» أَوْ «أَتَصَدَّقَ»، وَيَلْزَمُهُ مِنْ ذَلِكَ مَا يَقَعُ عَلَيْهِ الْاسْمُ. وَلَا نَذْرَ فِي مَعْصِيَةٍ كَقَوْلِهِ: «إِنْ قَتَلْتُ فُلَانًا فَلِلَّهِ عَلَيَّ كَذَا». وَلَا يَلْزَمُ النَّذْرُ عَلَى تَرْكِ مُبَاحٍ كَقَوْلِهِ: «لَا آكُلُ لَحْمًا» وَ«لَا أَشْرَبُ لَبَنًا» وَمَا أَشْبَهَ ذَلِكَ.

A vow to perform something that is lawful,[1] or an act of worship, that has been made contingent upon some event is binding. [It is]

1 This concerns lawful actions where there is some sort of natural incentive involved, such as reward. The final paragraph covers neutral actions.

like saying: "If Allah cures my patient, I owe Allah that I pray," or "...fast," or "...give charity."

What is required is anything given the same name [as what was mentioned].

Vows for acts of disobedience are not binding, such as saying: "If I murder so-and-so, I must do such-and-such."

Vows to abstain from [or to perform] something lawful [*mubāḥ*] are not binding, such as saying: "I will not eat meat, nor will I drink milk," and what resembles this.

16

COURTS AND TESTIMONY

كِتَابُ الْأَقْضِيَةِ وَالشَّهَادَاتِ

16.1 Judges

وَلَا يَجُوزُ أَنْ يَلِيَ الْقَضَاءَ إِلَّا مَنْ اسْتَكْمَلَتْ فِيهِ خَمْسَ عَشْرَةَ خَصْلَةً: الْإِسْلَامُ، وَالْبُلُوغُ، وَالْعَقْلُ، وَالْحُرِّيَّةُ، وَالذُّكُورِيَّةُ، وَالْعَدَالَةُ، وَمَعْرِفَةُ أَحْكَامِ الْكِتَابِ وَالسُّنَّةِ، وَمَعْرِفَةُ الْإِجْمَاعِ وَمَعْرِفَةُ الِاخْتِلَافِ، وَمَعْرِفَةُ طُرُقِ الِاجْتِهَادِ، وَمَعْرِفَةُ طَرَفٍ مِنْ لِسَانِ الْعَرَبِ وَمَعْرِفَةُ تَفْسِيرِ كِتَابِ اللهِ تَعَالَى، وَأَنْ يَكُونَ سَمِيعًا، وَأَنْ يَكُونَ بَصِيرًا، وَأَنْ يَكُونَ كَاتِبًا، وَأَنْ يَكُونَ مُسْتَيقِظًا.

It is not permissible for one to be appointed a judge unless he has fulfilled fifteen conditions. [The judge must:]

a. be a Muslim;
b. be mature;
c. be of sound mind;
d. be free;
e. be male;
f. be upright;
g. know the rulings from the Qur'ān and Sunnah;
h. know scholarly consensus;
i. know scholarly variance;
j. know the ways of independent reasoning;
k. know Arabic linguistics and philology, and explication of the Qur'ān;

l. possess eyesight;
m. possess hearing;
n. possess the ability to write;[1] and
o. be alert.

16.1.1 Etiquette

وَيُسْتَحَبُّ أَنْ يَجْلِسَ فِي وَسَطِ الْبَلَدِ فِي مَوْضِعٍ بَارِزٍ لِلنَّاسِ لَا حَاجِبَ لَهُ، وَلَا يَقْعُدُ لِلْقَضَاءِ فِي الْمَسْجِدِ. وَيُسَوِّي بَيْنَ الْخَصْمَيْنِ فِي ثَلَاثَةِ أَشْيَاءَ: فِي الْمَجْلِسِ، وَاللَّفْظِ، وَاللَّحْظِ. وَلَا يَجُوزُ أَنْ يَقْبَلَ الْهَدِيَّةَ مِنْ أَهْلِ عَمَلِهِ.

وَيَجْتَنِبُ الْقَضَاءَ فِي عَشَرَةِ مَوَاضِعَ: عِنْدَ الْغَضَبِ، وَالْجُوعِ، وَالْعَطَشِ، وَشِدَّةِ الشَّهْوَةِ، وَالْحُزْنِ، وَالْفَرَحِ الْمُفْرِطِ، وَالْمَرَضِ، وَمُدَافَعَةِ الْأَخْبَثَيْنِ، وَعِنْدَ النُّعَاسِ، وَشِدَّةِ الْحَرِّ وَالْبَرْدِ.

وَلَا يَسْأَلُ الْمُدَّعَى عَلَيْهِ إِلَّا بَعْدَ كَمَالِ الدَّعْوَى، وَلَا يُحَلِّفُهُ إِلَّا بَعْدَ سُؤَالِ الْمُدَّعِي. وَلَا يُلَقِّنُ خَصْمًا حُجَّةً، وَلَا يُفْهِمُهُ كَلَامًا، وَلَا يَتَعَنَّتُ بِالشُّهَدَاءِ.

وَلَا يَقْبَلُ الشَّهَادَةَ إِلَّا مِمَّنْ ثَبَتَتْ عَدَالَتُهُ. وَلَا يَقْبَلُ شَهَادَةَ عَدُوٍّ عَلَى عَدُوِّهِ، وَلَا شَهَادَةَ وَالِدٍ لِوَلَدِهِ، وَلَا وَلَدٍ لِوَالِدِهِ.

وَلَا يُقْبَلُ كِتَابُ قَاضٍ إِلَى قَاضٍ فِي الْأَحْكَامِ إِلَّا بَعْدَ شَهَادَةِ شَاهِدَيْنِ بِمَا فِيهِ.

It is recommended that the judge be situated in the middle of the region, in a place people can find with ease.

He should not have a doorman, and should not hold court within the mosque.

---

1 The sounder opinion is that it is not required that the judge know how to write.

The judge must treat both parties equally in three things:

1. where they sit;
2. how he addresses them; and
3. eye contact.

It is not permissible for him to accept a gift from people associated with his work.

He avoids deciding cases on ten occasions. When he:

1–3. is angry, hungry or thirsty;
4–6. feels sexual desire, sadness or joy to the extent that it causes negligence;
7. is sick;
8. needs to relieve himself;
9. is drowsy; or
10. is extremely hot or cold.

The judge does not question the defendant until the claim is complete, and he does not have the defendant swear an oath until the plaintiff asks.

He does not help either party formulate their proof against their opponent, nor does he explain how to make an allegation.

He does not badger the witnesses, nor accept testimony except from a witness whose uprightness has been established.

He does not accept an enemy testifying against his enemy, a son testifying for his father, or a father for his son.

A judge's written ruling that is sent to another judge is not accepted until two witnesses testify concerning its contents.

16.2 *Dividing Property*

(فَصْلٌ) وَيَفْتَقِرُ الْقَاسِمُ إِلَى سَبْعَةِ شَرَائِطَ: الْإِسْلَامُ، وَالْبُلُوغُ، وَالْعَقْلُ، وَالْحُرِّيَّةُ، وَالذُّكُورَةُ، وَالْعَدَالَةُ، وَالْحِسَابُ. فَإِنْ تَرَاضَى الشَّرِيكَانِ بِمَنْ يَقْسِمُ بَيْنَهُمَا لَمْ يَفْتَقِرْ إِلَى ذَلِكَ. وَإِنْ كَانَ فِي الْقِسْمَةِ تَقْوِيمٌ لَمْ يَقْتَصِرْ فِيهِ عَلَى أَقَلَّ مِنْ اثْنَيْنِ. وَإِذَا دَعَا أَحَدُ الشَّرِيكَيْنِ شَرِيكَهُ إِلَى قِسْمَةِ مَا لَا ضَرَرَ فِيهِ لَزِمَ الْآخَرَ.

Someone who divides [property for the court] must meet seven conditions. [The person must be:]

a. a Muslim;
b. mature;
c. of sound mind;
d. free;
e. male;
f. upright; and
g. trained in arithmetic.

If two [or more] parties agree that a particular person performs the division for them, the above conditions are not required.

If the division requires an assessment of value, there cannot be less than two appraisers.

If one partner invites the other partner to divide their property and there is no harm in doing so, he must comply.

16.3 *Evidence*

(فَصْلٌ) فَإِذَا كَانَ مَعَ الْمُدَّعِي بَيِّنَةٌ سَمِعَهَا الْحَاكِمُ وَحَكَمَ لَهُ بِهَا، فَإِنْ لَمْ يَكُنْ مَعَهُ بَيِّنَةٌ فَالْقَوْلُ قَوْلُ الْمُدَّعَى عَلَيْهِ بِيَمِينِهِ، فَإِنْ نَكَلَ الْمُدَّعَى عَلَيْهِ عَنِ الْيَمِينِ رُدَّتْ عَلَى الْمُدَّعِي فَيَحْلِفُ وَيَسْتَحِقُّ.

وَإِذَا تَدَاعَيَا شَيْئًا فِي يَدِ أَحَدِهِمَا، فَالْقَوْلُ قَوْلُ صَاحِبِ الْيَدِ بِيَمِينِهِ. وَإِنْ كَانَ فِي يَدِهِمَا تَحَالَفَا وَجُعِلَ بَيْنَهُمَا.

وَمَنْ حَلَفَ عَلَى فِعلِ نَفْسِهِ حَلَفَ عَلَى الْبَتِّ وَالْقَطْعِ، وَمَنْ حَلَفَ عَلَى فِعْلِ غَيْرِهِ فَإِنْ كَانَ إِثْبَاتًا حَلَفَ عَلَى الْبَتِّ وَالْقَطْعِ، وَإِنْ كَانَ نَفْيًا مُطْلَقًا حَلَفَ عَلَى نَفْيِ الْعِلْمِ.

If the plaintiff possesses testimonial evidence, the judge listens to it and judges according to it. If the plaintiff lacks testimonial evidence, then the defendant's word accompanied by his oath is relied upon. If the defendant refuses to swear an oath, [the burden] returns to the plaintiff who swears an oath and thereby deserves [whatever is claimed].

If both parties claim something that one of them has in his possession, the word of the one who possesses it combined with his oath is what is relied upon. If the contested item is in their joint possession, they both swear an oath and the item is divided between them.

Whosoever swears an oath about his actions [whether affirmative or negative] swears about it absolutely.

Whosoever swears an oath about another's actions: if he affirms their actions, then he swears about it absolutely; if he negates their actions, then he swears a negation of knowledge [of its occurrence].

16.4 Testimony

(فَصْلٌ) وَلَا تُقْبَلُ الشَّهَادَةُ إِلَّا مِمَّنِ اجْتَمَعَتْ فِيهِ خَمْسُ خِصَالٍ: الْإِسْلَامُ، وَالْبُلُوغُ، وَالْعَقْلُ، وَالْحُرِّيَّةُ، وَالْعَدَالَةُ.

وَلِلْعَدَالَةِ خَمْسَةُ شَرَائِطَ: أَنْ يَكُونَ مُجْتَنِبًا لِلْكَبَائِرِ، غَيْرَ مُصِرٍّ عَلَى الْقَلِيلِ مِنْ الصَّغَائِرِ، سَلِيمَ السَّرِيرَةِ، مَأْمُونًا عِنْدَ الْغَضَبِ، مُحَافِظًا عَلَى مُرُوءَةِ مِثْلِهِ.

Testimony is not accepted except from someone with five attributes. [One must be:]

a. a Muslim;
b. mature;
c. of sound mind;
d. free; and
e. upright.

There are five conditions for being upright. [One must:]

a. avoid [each of] the enormities [*kabā'ir*];
b. not persist in [even] a small amount of minor sins [*ṣaghā'ir*];
c. have sound beliefs;
d. restrain oneself when angry; and
e. adhere to the common standards of observant Muslims of one's time and place [*muru'ah*].

16.5 *Rights*

(فَصْلٌ) وَالْحُقُوقُ ضَرْبَانِ: حَقُّ اللهِ تَعَالَى، وَحَقُّ الآدَمِيِّ.

There are two types of rights:

1. rights owed Allah; and
2. rights owed to human beings.

16.5.1 Human Rights

فَأَمَّا حُقُوقُ الآدَمِيِّينَ فَثَلَاثَةُ أَضْرُبٍ: ضَرْبٌ لَا يُقْبَلُ فِيهِ إِلَّا شَاهِدَانِ ذَكَرَانِ وَهُوَ مَا لَا يُقْصَدُ مِنْهُ الْمَالُ وَيَطَّلِعُ عَلَيْهِ الرِّجَالُ، وَضَرْبٌ يُقْبَلُ فِيهِ شَاهِدَانِ أَوْ رَجُلٌ

وَامْرَأَتَانِ أَوْ شَاهِدٌ وَيَمِينُ الْمُدَّعِي وَهُوَ مَا كَانَ الْقَصْدُ مِنْهُ الْمَالَ، وَضَرْبٌ يُقْبَلُ فِيهِ شَاهِدَانِ أَوْ رَجُلٌ وَامْرَأَتَانِ أَوْ أَرْبَعُ نِسْوَةٍ، وَهُوَ مَا لَا يَطَّلِعُ عَلَيْهِ الرِّجَالُ.

[With respect to witnesses,] there are three types of rights owed humans:

1. *matters through which money is not sought and that are typical for men to observe*: only two male witnesses are accepted;
2. *matters through which money is sought*: two male witnesses, one male witness and two female witnesses, or one male witness and the plaintiff's sworn oath are accepted; and
3. *matters which are not typically observed by men*: two men, one man and two women, or four women are accepted.

16.5.2 Divine Rights

وَأَمَّا حُقُوقُ اللهِ تَعَالَى فَلَا تُقْبَلُ فِيهَا النِّسَاءُ، وَهِيَ عَلَى ثَلَاثَةِ أَضْرُبٍ: ضَرْبٌ لَا يُقْبَلُ فِيهِ أَقَلُّ مِنْ أَرْبَعَةٍ وَهُوَ الزِّنَا، وَضَرْبٌ يُقْبَلُ فِيهِ اثْنَانِ وَهُوَ مَا سِوَى الزِّنَا مِنَ الْحُدُودِ، وَضَرْبٌ يُقْبَلُ فِيهِ وَاحِدٌ وَهُوَ هِلَالُ شَهْرِ رَمَضَانَ.

A woman's testimony is never accepted for rights owed Allah.

[With respect to witnesses,] there are three types of rights owed Allah:

1. *fornication*: less than four male witnesses are never accepted;
2. *punishments other than fornication*: two male witnesses are accepted; and
3. *sighting the crescent moon at the beginning of Ramadan*: one individual male witness is accepted.

16.5.3 Inadmissible Testimony

وَلَا تُقْبَلُ شَهَادَةُ الْأَعْمَى إِلَّا فِي سِتَّةِ مَوَاضِعَ: الْمَوْتُ، وَالنَّسَبُ، وَالْمِلْكُ الْمُطْلَقُ، وَالتَّرْجَمَةُ، وَمَا شَهِدَ بِهِ قَبْلَ الْعَمَى، وَعَلَى الْمَضْبُوطِ.

وَلَا تُقْبَلُ شَهَادَةُ جَارٍّ لِنَفْسِهِ نَفْعًا وَلَا دَافِعٍ عَنْهَا ضَرَرًا.

Testimony from a blind witness is inadmissible except in five cases:

1. death;
2. lineage;
3. general ownership;
4. translation; and
5. things witnessed before becoming blind; and, for example, when someone tells him something and he immediately takes the speaker by the hand in order to present him to the judge and testify as to what was said.

It is not permissible for anyone to provide testimony through which personal benefit is derived or personal harm is warded off.

17

MANUMISSION

كِتَابُ الْعِتْقِ

17.1 *Manumission of Slaves*

وَيَصِحُّ الْعِتْقُ مِنْ كُلِّ مَالِكٍ جَائِزِ التَّصَرُّفِ فِي مِلْكِهِ، وَيَقَعُ الْعِتْقُ بِصَرِيحِ الْعِتْقِ وَالْكِنَايَةِ مَعَ النِّيَّةِ. وَإِذا أَعْتَقَ بَعْضَ عَبْدٍ عَتَقَ جَمِيعُهُ. وَإِنْ أَعْتَقَ شِرْكًا لَهُ فِي عَبْدٍ وَهُوَ مُوسِرٌ سَرَى الْعِتْقُ إِلَى بَاقِيهِ وَكَانَ عَلَيْهِ قِيمَةُ نَصِيبِ شَرِيكِهِ.

وَمَنْ مَلَكَ وَاحِدًا مِنْ وَالِدِيهِ أَوْ مَوْلُودِهِ عَتَقَ عَلَيْهِ.

Manumission is valid from every slave owner who is entitled to dispose of his own property.[1]

Manumission occurs through an explicit phrase, or an allusive phrase accompanied by intention.

The entire slave is set free when the owner frees [just] a portion. When a co-owner frees his portion of a slave: if he is not poor, the manumission extends to the entire slave and he must pay the value of his partners' portions [to his partners].

When one takes possession of his own parents or children, [the relative] is automatically set free.

1 See "7.7 Suspension" on page 69.

17.2 *Walā'*

(فَصْلٌ) وَالْوَلَاءُ مِنْ حُقُوقِ الْعِتْقِ، وَحُكْمُهُ حُكْمُ التَّعْصِيبِ عِنْدَ عَدَمِهِ. وَيَنْتَقِلُ الْوَلَاءُ عَنِ الْمُعْتِقِ إِلَى الذُّكُورِ مِنْ عَصَبَتِهِ. وَتَرْتِيبُ الْعَصَبَاتِ فِي الْوَلَاءِ كَتَرْتِيبِهِمْ فِي الْإِرْثِ، وَلَا يَجُوزُ بَيْعُ الْوَلَاءِ وَلَا هِبَتُهُ.

Walā' is a right [associated with] manumission. Its ruling is akin to the [inheritance] ruling in the absence of the deceased's universal inheritor.[2] [Upon death,] *walā'* passes from the one who freed the slave to the [deceased's] male universal inheritors; the order for universal inheritors here is as their order for inheritance.

It is not permissible to sell *walā'*, nor to give it as a gift.

17.3 *Stipulating Freedom Upon Death*

(فَصْلٌ) وَمَنْ قَالَ لِعَبْدِهِ: «إِذَا مِتُّ فَأَنْتَ حُرٌّ»، فَهُوَ مُدَبَّرٌ يَعْتِقُ بَعْدَ وَفَاتِهِ مِنْ ثُلُثِهِ. وَيَجُوزُ لَهُ أَنْ يَبِيعَهُ فِي حَالِ حَيَاتِهِ وَيَبْطُلُ تَدْبِيرُهُ. وَحُكْمُ الْمُدَبَّرِ فِي حَالِ حَيَاةِ السَّيِّدِ حُكْمُ الْعَبْدِ الْقِنِّ.

If the owner tells his slave, "You are free upon my death," the slave becomes a *mudabbar*; he is set free upon his master's death, from [the top] one-third of the estate.

It is permissible for the owner to sell the slave while he is alive. Selling the slave invalidates the slave being set free upon the owner's death.

A slave who will be set free upon his owner's death is the same as a fully-owned slave.

2 See "8.1.5 Universal Inheritors" on page 89.

17.4 *Buying One's Freedom*

(فَصْلٌ) وَالْكِتَابَةُ مُسْتَحَبَّةٌ إِذَا سَأَلَهَا الْعَبْدُ وَكَانَ مَأْمُونًا مُكْتَسِبًا. وَلَا تَصِحُّ إِلَّا بِمَالٍ مَعْلُومٍ، ويكونُ مُؤَجَّلًا إِلَى أَجَلٍ مَعْلُومٍ، وَأَقَلُّهُ نَجْمَانِ. وَهِيَ مِنْ جِهَةِ السَّيِّدِ لَازِمَةٌ، وَمِنْ جِهَةِ الْعَبْدِ الْمُكَاتَبِ جَائِزَةٌ فَلَهُ فَسْخُهَا مَتَى شَاءَ.

وَلِلْمُكَاتَبِ التَّصَرُّفُ فِيمَا فِي يَدِهِ مِنَ الْمَالِ. وَعَلَى السَّيِّدِ أَنْ يَضَعَ مِنْ مَالِ الْكِتَابَةِ مَا يَسْتَعِينُ بِهِ عَلَى أَدَاءِ نُجُومِ الْكِتَابَةِ، وَلَا يَعْتِقُ إِلَّا بَعْدَ أَدَاءِ جَمِيعِ الْمَالِ.

If a slave requests to purchase his freedom [*kitābah*], it is recommended that the owner accept the request if the slave is trustworthy and employed. The contract is not valid unless there is a specified amount that is deferred to a known date. The amount must be paid in at least two installments.

The owner cannot revoke the contract, although the slave is entitled to do so whenever he wishes.

A slave who is purchasing his freedom is entitled to dispose of property in his possession.[3]

It is obligatory for the owner to reduce a portion of the manumission price so that the slave can use it to help pay the installments.

The slave is not set free until he has paid the price in full.

3 He is restricted, however, to engaging in transactions that are likely to bring about an increase in the overall value of his property.

17.5 *Umm al-Walad*

(فَصْلٌ) وَإِذَا أَصَابَ السَّيِّدُ أَمَتَهُ فَوَضَعَتْ مَا يَتَبَيَّنُ فِيهِ شَيْءٌ مِنْ خَلْقِ آدَمِيٍّ، حَرُمَ عَلَيْهِ بَيْعُهَا وَرَهْنُهَا وَهِبَتُهَا وَجَازَ لَهُ التَّصَرُّفُ فِيهَا بِالِاسْتِخْدَامِ وَالْوَطْءِ، وَإِذَا مَاتَ السَّيِّدُ عَتَقَتْ مِنْ رَأْسِ مَالِهِ قَبْلَ الدُّيُونِ وَالْوَصَايَا، وَوَلَدُهَا مِنْ غَيْرِهِ بِمَنْزِلَتِهَا.

وَمَنْ أَصَابَ أَمَةَ غَيْرِهِ بِنِكَاحٍ فَوَلَدُهُ مِنْهَا مَمْلُوكٌ لِسَيِّدِهَا. فَإِنْ أَصَابَهَا بِشُبْهَةٍ فَوَلَدُهُ مِنْهَا حُرٌّ، وَعَلَيْهِ قِيمَتُهُ لِلسَّيِّدِ. وَإِنْ مَلَكَ الْأَمَةَ الْمُطَلَّقَةَ بَعْدَ ذَلِكَ لَمْ تَصِرْ أُمَّ وَلَدٍ بِالْوَطْءِ فِي النِّكَاحِ، وَصَارَتْ أُمَّ وَلَدٍ بِالْوَطْءِ بِالشُّبْهَةِ عَلَى أَحَدِ الْقَوْلَيْنِ.

If a slave owner impregnates his slave and she gives birth to something resembling a human being, [she becomes an *umm al-walad*] and he may not sell her, use her as collateral or give her as a gift.

He may put her to work [i.e., hire her out] and have sex with her.

When he dies, she is set free from the top of the estate before the payment of debts and distribution of bequests.

Her child from another man [after giving birth to her master's child] follows her in this ruling.[4]

Whoever impregnates his wife who is another person's slave, the child becomes the property of the owner.

If one impregnates a slave through dubious intercourse, his child from her is free and he must pay its value to the master.[5]

If he purchases a slave [to whom] he [was previously married and

4 Thus, if she bears a child through marriage or fornication, that child is set free with her.

5 Examples of dubious intercourse include the master mistaking someone else's slave for his own wife or his own slave.

then] divorced after she had given birth to his child, she does not become an *umm al-walad* through him having had intercourse with her while married. But according to one opinion, she does if he had dubious intercourse with her.[6]

وَاللهُ أَعْلَمُ.

And Allah knows best.

6 The other opinion is that she does not become his *umm walad*; it is the preponderant ruling.

BIBLIOGRAPHY

المَصَادِرُ وَالمَرَاجِعُ

Abū Shujā' al-Aṣfahānī, Aḥmad ibn al-Ḥusayn. *Matn Ghāyat al-Taqrīb.* Edited and annotated by 'Alawī Abū Bakr Muḥammad al-Saqqāf. Jakarta: Dār al-Kutub al-Islāmīyah, 1423 AH/2003 CE.

——, and Abū al-Faḍl Walī al-Dīn al-Baṣīr. *Al-Nihāya.* 2nd ed. Cairo: Maṭba'ah al-Istīqāmah, n.d.

——, Ibrāhīm ibn Muḥammad al-Bājūrī, and Muḥammad ibn Qāsim al-Ghazzī. *Ḥāshiyat al-Shaykh Ibrāhīm al-Bayjūrī* [sic] *'alā Sharḥ al-'Allāmah Ibn Qāsim al-Ghazzī 'alā Matn al-Shaykh Abī Shujā'.* 2 vols. Beirut: Dār Iḥyā' al-Turāth al-'Arabī, 2002.

——, and Muḥammad al-Khaṭīb al-Sharbīnī. *Al-Iqnā' fī Ḥall Alfāẓ Abī Shujā'.* 2 vols. Damascus: Dār al-Khayr: 1423 AH/2002 CE.

——, Muḥammad ibn Qāsim al-Ghazzī, and Muḥammad al-Nawawī al-Jāwī. *Qūt al-Ḥabīb al-Gharīb.* Cairo: Maṭba' Muṣṭafā al-Bābī al-Ḥalabī, 1357 AH/1938 CE.

——, and Muṣṭafā al-Bughā. *Al-Tahdhīb fī Adillat Matn al-Ghāyat wa-l-Taqrīb.* Beirut: Dār al-Fikr, 1412 AH/1992 CE.

——, Taqī al-Dīn Muḥammad al-Ḥuṣnī al-Ḥusaynī. *Kifāyat al-akhyār fī Ḥall Ghāyat al-Ikhtiṣār fī al-Fiqh al-Shāfi'ī.* Edited by 'Abd al-Qādir al-Arnā'ūṭ. Damascus: Dār al-Khayr, 1418 AH/1998 CE.

——, Shihāb al-Dīn Aḥmad al-Fashnī, and Yaḥyā ibn Nūr al-Dīn al-'Amarītī. *Tahdhīb Tuḥfat al-Ḥabīb fī Sharh Nihāyat al-Tadrīb.* Edited by Qāsim al-Nūrī. Damascus: u.k., 1996.

INDEX

conditions 11
duration 11
invalidators 12
Khul[c] 105
Legal responsibility 21
Looking at the opposite sex 97
Lost items 83
Major ritual impurity 18
Manumission 157. *See also* Slaves
buying one's freedom 159
stipulating upon death 158
walā' 158
Marriage. *See also* Financial support
conditions 98
engagement 99
guardians 98, 99
integrals 98
looking at the opposite sex 97
marriage payment 102
marrying slaves 96
people who should marry 96
spousal defects 102
wedding feast 103
witnesses 98
wives
disobedience 104
giving equal time 104
number of 96
women
compulsion 100
unmarriageable 100
Menstruation
actions unlawful during 18
See also Irregular bleeding 16
Minor ritual impurity 19
Miswāk 5
Mudabbar 158
Mukātabah 159
Non-Muslim Residents 136
Non-Muslims
indemnity 123
Oaths. *See also* Vows
binding phrases 146
thoughtless 146
Objects
gold 4
silver 4
People of the Book 136
animals slaughtered by 140
Pilgrimage. *See also* Sacred Precinct
conditions obligating 58
Ḥajj
expiation 62
integrals 58
obligatory actions 59
omissions during 61
recommended actions 60
things unlawful during 60
ʿUmrah
integrals 59
Postnatal bleeding
actions unlawful during 18
Prayer. *See also* Clothes; *See also* Friday Prayer; *See also* Funerals
actions
combining 32
during peril 38
inability to stand 29
integrals 23
quantity of elements 28
recommended prior to prayer 25
recommended within prayer, lesser 25
recommended within prayer, major 25
shortening 32
conditions
for it being obligatory 21
prerequisites 23
Congregational prayer 31
Drought Prayer 36
Eclipse Prayer 36
forgetfulness 29
invalidators 28
punishment for omitting 132
recommended prayers 21
Midmorning 22
Night Vigil 22
rawātib 22
Tarawih 22
Witr 22
times 20

guarantees
payment 72
physical presence 73
impermissible transactions 67
lending 76
lost items 83
offering collateral 69
ordering goods 68
partnerships 73
preemption 77
reconciliation 70
renting goods and hiring services 80
reviving abandoned lands 81
sharecropping 81
types 65
wages 80
watering crops 79
water rights 82
wrongfully-taken property 77
Travelers
combining prayers 32
fasting 56
shortening prayers 32
ʿUmrah 59
Unlawful gain 66
Vows. *See also* Oaths
abstaining from the lawful 148
acts of disobedience 148
acts of worship 147
expiation 147
lawful acts 147, 148
spiritual retreat 57
Walā' 158
Walīmah 103
Waqf 82
Water
categories 3
rights 82
Wills 94
Women
and fasting 56
and prayer 27
indemnity 123
marriage and compulsion 100
Wuḍūʿ 5
Zakāh
agriculture 46, 49
cows 47
distributing 51
fruit 46, 49
goats 48
gold and silver 49
impermissible recipients 51
livestock 44
mixed flocks 48
money 45
ore 50
sheep 48
trade goods 46, 50
treasure 50
types 44
Zakāt al-Fitr 50
Ẓihār 109

Printed by Amazon Italia Logistica S.r.l.
Torrazza Piemonte (TO), Italy

12888549R00105